Praise for Vince Benevento

"Vince found his purpose in working with young men to protect and nurture their growth and heal their mental health and wellbeing. He is a master at what he does, and the impact of his work on his community and his patients is nothing short of extraordinary. Helping young men navigate the modern world and the evolving picture of masculinity is complicated work, and Vince delivers his message in bold but accessible prose guided by both empathy and humanity. Now with his lessons in print, Vince's teachings can reach the millions of men and their families and friends who can benefit from his learnings. If someone you love is struggling, this book will help them navigate their struggles and will help you better understand all the ways that you can help love them through it."

—David Stone, Cofounder, TFC Management and TFC Productions

"Our school has been blessed to collaborate with Vince for many years. He has been an energetic and positive presence, whether leading impactful full-student presentations, working with small groups, or engaging thoughtfully with our parents. His dedication to young men's mental health and his care for the whole person align beautifully with our Jesuit values. We are deeply grateful for his partnership and the way he has enriched our community."

—Timothy G. Dee, Principal, Fairfield College Preparatory School

"Every time I sit and connect with Vince, I'm always left in awe of his passion, conviction, dedication, and creativity. Vince has dedicated his life to serving others, and through his vast experience, he's often able to predict the positive trajectory of the lives he's able to touch. In today's world, the clear-cut solution toward betterment is often lost in the overwhelm of information overload. Vince's approach has always been filled with heart, love, empathy, and understanding. Growing up in today's society isn't easy, and it typically takes a village. Vince has helped architect villages of support around the world, and now with a codified blueprint, he will continue to serve, as he always has."

—Jamie Hazelton, Executive Vice President, Turnbridge

"No one understands the challenges facing young men on the brink of adulthood better than Vince Benevento. His insight, compassion, and unwavering guidance have helped countless clients find their footing—and it has been a privilege to collaborate with him in supporting these life-changing transitions. He brings unparalleled wisdom and heart to the complex process of helping young men step into their future."

—Chris Bogart, Founder, Sasco River Center

"Collaborating with Vince Benevento and Causeway Collaborative has been both inspiring and impactful. Vince's commitment to young men's mental health aligns deeply with my own mission, and together we've worked to elevate the conversation around emotional wellbeing, purpose, and growth. His innovative, team-based approach continues to make a meaningful difference in the lives of the families we serve."

—Marc Lehman, Founder, U Are Heard, and Podcaster/Founder, *Normalize It Forward* podcast

"Vince has dedicated his life to helping young men who are searching for direction, and the impact of his work is nothing short of extraordinary. For years, I've watched him guide those who are struggling with motivation, academics, or substance use, and he consistently brings out the best in them. His compassion, his practical wisdom, and his ability to connect with both young men and their families have transformed hundreds of lives. The book he has written is a reflection of all that experience—a roadmap built from real-world successes, challenges, and lessons that have stood the test of time. This book is not only inspiring, it's actionable. Vince translates his proven approach into guidance that young men and their parents can put to work immediately. It's filled with insights that foster accountability, resilience, and a renewed sense of purpose, written in a way that feels supportive rather than prescriptive. For anyone seeking hope and a clear path forward, this book is an invaluable resource. I wholeheartedly recommend it, and I believe it will continue the ripple effect of change Vince has been creating for years."

—Max Rosenthal, Chief People Officer, leading asset management firm

BOYS WILL BE MEN

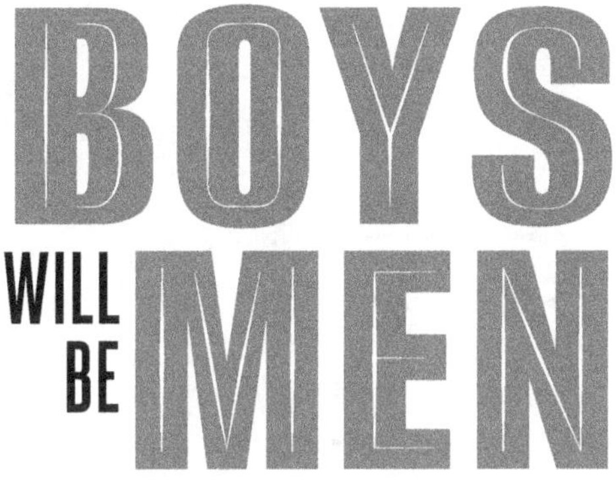

8 Lessons for the Lost American Male

Vince Benevento

MERIDIAN EDITIONS
WESTPORT, CONNECTICUT

Published by Meridian Editions
Westport, Connecticut

www.meridianeditions.com

ISBN (paperback): 978-1-959170-31-0
ISBN (hardcover): 978-1-959170-30-3
ISBN (ebook): 978-1-959170-32-7

Cover and book designed by John Lotte

Manufactured in the U.S.A.

To Leo

For teaching me that the lions and bears that we fight along the way exist to prepare us for the Giants we haven't met yet

CONTENTS

INTRODUCTION

Who am I and why should you listen to me?

Therapy is largely useless for young men ages sixteen to thirty. Or, to put it less harshly, talk therapy (in isolation) for young men just doesn't work.

I say this despite being a licensed therapist for more than ten years and the founder of Causeway Collaborative, a counseling center for men and young men. I have owned and run the organization for the last thirteen years plus, and it has grown from a single-man shop to three therapeutic centers spanning across two states and a team of more than twenty-five individuals.

I say this now at age forty-three, looking back on myself as a young man who needed a lot more help. During my senior year in high school and my first three years at Wesleyan University, I was a binge drinker—it consumed nearly every free moment of my life. I was also plagued by severe mental health issues that would eventually manifest in the form of a lifelong mental health diagnosis.

I say this despite having been in therapy for most of my adult life.

I say this as a man who's been married for almost seventeen years to Gina, the love of my life—a man whose marriage almost didn't survive the long and winding road I've traversed.

I say this as the father of two boys, Vince and Leo, who I hope and pray will grow up into young men who don't require extraordinary professional help measures like their father before them.

I say this as a father to Giovanna, my little princess, who helped me learn how to seek her heart and my love for her in ways she needed.

What does work for young men?

In order to do the work that I imagined, with the population that I was pulled toward—young men ages sixteen to thirty—I needed a form of therapeutic support that *does* work.

What does work? Based upon my background, lived experience, and learning, what works is the unique, action-focused approach to working with young men that we've developed and honed at the organization I started, Causeway Collaborative. We've identified a new and different approach to working with young men for over thirteen years. We've given them choices; we've heard their perspectives; we've identified what motivates them; and we've built a plan on the foundation of the goals they have for their own lives. To do so, we've relied on different kinds of services and a fresh approach to working with men and young men.

We help model appropriate behaviors for men through

experiential therapy: Therapeutic Mentorship. Here, our clinicians partner with a young man to teach him life skills, which helps strengthen his interpersonal proficiencies and **introduces him to his inner Wild.**

For a young man who possesses the readiness to better understand himself and gain insight, our solution-focused version of therapy **drives a young man to know and accept himself (even the ugly parts).**

Our proprietary approach to career and academic support, Futures Planning, helps a young man navigate school and career goals to identify a long-term vision for his future, and then equips him with the tangible skills to achieve personal goals week over week. In sum, we help young men **find their thing and chase it with all they have.**

Finally, through Family Coaching, for those brave families willing to take the invitation to do the work alongside their son, we impart practical strategies parents can use to be more present in their son's life. We impress upon them that **provision is not a substitute for presence,** and no amount of money and success can replace them being a present force in the life of their son.

This kind of therapy could have saved me from myself

It is precisely those ideal circumstances—a novel, refreshing, multidimensional approach to therapy—that potentially could have saved me so much emotional difficulty and pain when I was a young man.

I started struggling in the late 1990s and early 2000s with both mental health and substance use issues. At the time, I was your stereotypical meathead jock in high school. I'd go out on the weekend, get drunk, chase girls, and screw around—that was just what guys like me did back then.

But at that point, my family was imploding. So much so that during the last semester of my senior year of high school, I was getting drunk every single day and never going to class.

I was nineteen years old, a disaster, and very sick

I hobbled across the finish line in high school and found my way to the very respectable Wesleyan University as a consolation prize.

But when I arrived home that first summer, I became severely depressed. Think bedridden depressed. As I battled the onset of my severe depressive episode, I did things that felt good in the moment but escalated my symptoms and my isolative tendencies. I stopped engaging with my friends, communicating with my family, and even carrying out basic hygiene practices. I was nineteen years old, a disaster, and very sick.

It got so bad that I had thoughts of ending my life. As a result, I was hospitalized during the summer before my sophomore year of college. At that time, I hated myself and hated my life.

At the hospital, they recalibrated my meds and sent me on my way after a nearly ten-day stint.

A month later, I went back to college and locked myself in my room for three days. I didn't eat, wouldn't see friends, and refused to answer my door. Crippling anxiety left me so ill-equipped to function that I was barely able to exist, let alone thrive as a student on a college campus. Concerned friends alerted the authorities on campus to my struggles, and soon after, Public Safety kicked my door in and extracted me from my off-campus apartment. From there, the only possible option was to take the semester off as a medical leave of absence.

Years finding my way led me to start Causeway Collaborative

It took years for me to find my way from being a mentally ill college kid who had recently been hospitalized to becoming a young man who cared about things and had a vision for his life. But despite the pain in my heart and the noise in my mind, there was a spark within me. That spark was fanned through years of finding my way and eventually became the passion and fire behind Causeway Collaborative.

Causeway provides a space for men to identify a quest, encounter hardships, find a passion along the way, and continue to test themselves until they emerge as better, more certain, and more clear. However, that journey can never occur in isolation. On the hero's quest, a young man will require the **essential support that only forming relationships with other men can provide.**

We have inspired young men for more than thirteen years to run toward new situations, head-on, and be willing to try, fail, and keep going—to journey into the unknown, face novel circumstances, and be invigorated by personal challenge. We teach them, **"Never tap out. Ever."**

We sharpen young men. We hold young men to account,

providing them with direct feedback, and we aren't afraid to tell it like it is. **Unfortunately, sometimes we're forced to do so in the absence of their own fathers.**

We, alongside our clients, **aren't afraid to make a mess, and we aren't afraid to clean it up, either.** We model for young men a bygone way of doing things: to do a hard thing, continue trying it until you improve and eventually succeed, and then move toward the next hard thing on your way to something beautiful of your own design.

We've moved the needle

A long time ago, we set out to change the way mental health care is done for men and young men.

Doing it our way meant committing our professional lives to accomplishing that goal. In many ways, we've already done it. We have the data to support it, the customer satisfaction scores to prove it worked, and enough of a historical census to demonstrate that we've moved the needle toward accomplishing that goal. Now, doing it our way for real means we have to make sure as many people as possible know about our approach to helping men and young men and can use it to educate themselves and improve the lives of their sons in the process.

At forty-three, I run the largest all-male outpatient counseling center in the Northeast. Causeway Collaborative serves only male clients, with more than twenty-five practitioners across three locations. We've supported more than 2,500 families over thirteen years by coaching and developing independent, healthy, and capable young men. I've learned how to be a businessman somewhere along this road, too. But in my opinion, our success is due primarily to the unique ways in which we approach treatment, coaching, and counseling for treatment-resistant young men.

So examine the road I've traveled ... the road ahead for boys and men

So read on. Read on and learn how I worked to become a better version of myself along this bumpy and winding road and how I grew in my understanding of how to better support young men in the process.

If you do, you'll learn about new methods to help the young men of Gen Z. You'll also hear stories of the issues that all young men of this generation face, as well as the generation of millennial men prior. You'll undoubtedly see the common ground that they share with the boys and men in your life. Finally, and most importantly, you'll learn **eight practical life lessons that men of all ages can implement to become better versions of themselves,** taken directly from the personal experience of a life spent in service to young men.

What's happening with young men?

In the last decade, I've noticed a massive sociological shift in young men and their families. Ten years ago, millennial teens who came to Causeway Collaborative acted out in ways that I connected with, and that made sense to me. Their struggles paralleled my own. They drove their cars fast, drank to excess, got into fistfights, got arrested, and generally engaged in behavior that scared the hell out of their parents. Back then, it was easy to identify a "Causeway Guy" because a decade ago, when a kid came in to see me, typically their world was on fire.

As a result, two things were true: First, parents actually listened to us. At least me. When your kid is doing dangerous and risky things, you listen to the experts because the situation is critical. But from a risk perspective, the young men who come through these days are not requiring urgent help anymore. Most of them are anxious, depressed, isolated video gamers who smoke pot and don't really do much else. That's a pain to manage, but certainly not a true risk. Often, in fact, parents have understood that a problem exists, but they haven't addressed it for years on end. Parents think because there is no true risk, maybe things will resolve of their own accord. Typically, that's not the case.

Second, parents used to prioritize getting their kids launched and out of the house. But these days, we're not in the launch business anymore. We're in the "peaceful cohabitation business." Young men live at home longer. They don't date as much, so they don't get married. They take longer to graduate from college, which means they take longer to get their first jobs, if they get a job at all. COVID-19 changed everything and accelerated a growing culture of fear, both for parents and for the young men who reside in their basements. As a result, parents are concerned about their kids' safety and wellbeing and would rather keep these kids under their watchful eyes at home than in their own place. Out on their own, they would be more independent, yes, but potentially more lonely and isolated. Right now, in our country, the number one issue facing men and young men isn't substance use; it's not even mental health. It's loneliness. And parents know this now—even if they're not able to devise a plan for how to react to what they observe.

Despite their best intentions, one unintended side effect of this trend toward more active parental support beyond high school is that somewhere along this parental road, parents started prioritizing their kids' comfort over holding them accountable. This has roots in the mental health crisis, built on a growing awareness of how much young people truly are struggling with their emotions and their mental health, coupled with a better fundamental awareness of the myriad of ways that mental illness manifests itself: anxiety, depression, substance use, school refusal, self-harm, video game addiction—just to name a few. It may also stem from a general societal malaise around misgivings concerning what, in fact, is in the best interest of young men. Right now, Gen Z is suffering more than any generation of young men in human history, but because these struggles are more chronic than acute, it's unclear to most parents what precisely to do to effectively support their sons.

The truth is, when parents restrict their sons of any age from accomplishing age-appropriate developmental milestones, the prevailing message received is, "Son, you're not capable." Instead, the message must be recalibrated and shifted to, "Son, because I love you and I know that you're far more capable than what you're demonstrating at present, here is what I have to do as your parent …" This shift toward comfort-focused parenting and away from parenting by joint consensus and accountability makes our work as therapists and coaches much more complicated and multidimensional.

I was a "Causeway of Old" type in my youth—drinking, drugging, drinking and driving, fighting, getting arrested—a young man who frequently did dangerous and risky things. It might seem that the modern "Causeway Guy" and his behaviors are not as problematic. However, the truth is that his issues are biologically activated by the same unique command centers of the brain that were stimulated in his substance-using counterparts.

Ironically, in many ways I'd assert that the modern equivalent is in fact worse. For the young men of today, stimulation itself *is* their drug. They *need* to be plugged in. They *need* to be actively consuming content and stimulation. Absent those inputs, many young men don't know how to function. Their brain is so perpetually flooded with stimuli that to be still for a second feels impossible to them. Their socialization is largely relegated to pack-based competition in an artificial world that nonetheless feels surprisingly real and also matters tremendously in ways that parents or, more broadly, adults simply can't connect with. Oftentimes because of their own frustration, parents don't even try to get it. Most can't, despite how hard they try.

Again, at a cursory glance, the second type of guy—the Gen Z male—represents significantly fewer risk factors than his predecessors. There's usually no threat of legal involvement. Given the perpetual abstinence from sex that comes alongside this profile, there is certainly no risk of getting someone pregnant. These guys don't engage in substance use to the same degree; they don't stay out past curfew; and because they are not navigating the demands of the world around them in the same fashion, they don't feel compelled to lie to cover their tracks since there aren't any tracks to begin with. Nor is there a need to manipulate others for their own gain. Seems like a significant improvement from their harder-charging millennial predecessors. Maybe guys aren't trending in the wrong direction after all?

But I would argue that what I see with today's population of Gen Z males is worse. Back in the day, I had a girlfriend.

I had a job. I played sports. I saved money and bought my own car with the aid of the job that I worked. I had friends who I interacted with in person and saw daily, even outside of school. Yes, I was a disaster in many and most ways, but I was lapping today's young man in ways that I would argue are far more important: relational formation, delayed gratification, persistence, work ethic, interpersonal skills, and daily structure.

Today's young man is also allergic to healthy risk-taking. He is far too reliant on his parents to do for him what he can easily do for himself. He has constructed a sort of virtual cocoon to keep himself fully insulated from healthy prosocial relationships, trial, failure, and iteration. This man-boy is simulating his own adventure instead of seeking it in the way that all previous cultures helped usher men into adulthood through a combination of ritual, mentorship, role modeling, and trial and error. The actions of his predecessors (substance use, promiscuity, legal involvement, educational disengagement) were significant issues, sure, particularly in the business that I built, grew, and have run for the past thirteen years. But I see these new challenges as far more dire and far more urgent in their escalating need. Worst of all, these issues exist absent a singular and shared societal belief that these are critically urgent situations in the way that I am clamoring for them to be identified.

Young men of today need a new approach to provide effective support. They are far too unmotivated, confused, distracted, and unwell to both do it on their own and do it through conventional means. The chronic nature of their apathy coupled with their lack of vision for a positive and sustainable future makes them incredibly hard to inspire, and it's even more difficult to render them ongoing support without them opting out. They are not behaving dangerously enough to require a higher level of care (a.k.a. hospitalization or inpatient residential stay) but require more intensive care than to rely upon conventional means, like once-per-week talk therapy. In truth, they are flying below the radar of the level of support that would prove effective in helping them address, move through, and solve their issues once and for all.

In sum, I'm here to be a message bearer: We're in deep trouble. We don't know quite how bad yet because we still don't completely understand the scope of the damage already done to the men and young men of this generation. But if we don't fix this problem in both profound and surgically efficient ways with *this* generation, our society is going to be in very serious trouble.

Who is this book for?

This book is for the young man or man who wants to take the wheel in driving his own life forward. Who isn't afraid to begin to do the work. Who can be honest with himself about the way things look. And who is brave enough to take any step forward, view it as a start of something positive, and learn a lesson that may prove useful.

I'm here to share my personal experiences with you. I have very few answers, only stories that illustrate how my perspective has changed over time. I was a "Causeway of Old" type as a young man; as such, over the years I have thought long and hard about what I needed to do differently to show up as a different version of myself once I understood how serious my problems were. This exact principle is why I started my own business, benchmarking novel service types based on what would have resonated with a younger version of myself. Now, I hope to do the same thing in sharing my life's work with anyone who is a struggling man or young man.

To do so, I've gathered some of my truest and most representative examples of the types of change that young men can make when they commit to a process, do the work, and trust the mentor and coach who is guiding them on that journey. I've connected those stories with my own experiences to show trials and successes that drive the point home. I've also worked to boil those takeaways down to a singular lesson in each chapter. This will allow you to more effectively share ideas with others, in an effort to both further your own learning as well as to mentor someone else who could use your support.

But this book is also for parents. As a parent of three myself, I see now that my role in my kids' lives has never been more necessary. I've seen parents attempt to navigate their role across a broad continuum over the last fifteen years, from guys I regard as some of the finest men and dads I've ever met to moms and dads who have done such a bad job as parents that they've irreparably damaged their sons. Personally, like most others, there are some things I got right along the way and some things I wish I could take back.

Overall, as a guy who's been a father for more than thirteen years, I became a good dad over time—like my former teenage self, who course-corrected and did things differently. I tried. Failed. Iterated. Failed again. Eventually, by getting things wrong and by changing how I responded to the daily crises of varying degrees associated with raising children, I became more effective at fathering, mostly by being open to parenting each of my kids as unique individuals. I want to speak specifically to moms and dads to reinforce for them how much their influence matters as well as share with them some stories, advice, and perspective to help them navigate their own journeys as they wade through the muck of modern parenting.

Finally, this book is specifically for husbands. In my work to explore my own issues and remain balanced as I have helped young men, I've also healed my marriage. I've tried to separate myself and the story in this book from the story of my wife and me, but I simply can't. She is core to who I am and has walked alongside me at every step of this road, both good and bad. I can't tell the story of me without making this a story of Vince and Gina. Practically speaking, part of our interconnectedness comes from her being my CFO and business partner for the past eight years. But separate from that, we have our own story to tell here, which may help others as well. Husbands, I hope my story is useful to you as you pursue the heart of the partner in your life.

So this is it. This is my life's work, how we built it, how we fixed it, and lessons learned from it. Much of this came from being transparent with myself and unapologetically sharing those lessons along the way.

LESSON 1

Brick by Brick

MEN NEED TO BUILD THINGS. I've always known this. I used to sit and watch my boys building block towers as toddlers. I would do this for hours. They would stack them up as high as they could, only to have them inevitably fall over. But when they would, my boys would jump up, only to start again, relentlessly trying to get their towers to grow taller than the previous time. I marveled at their persistence.

We see this, too, as boys assemble into teams on the playground. When captains are chosen and classrooms are divided, each young man is vying to build the best possible recess roster ever constructed, using the requisite pieces at one's disposal. In sum, it's an evolutionary game of conquest of epic proportion, each young man competing for superiority and to build something special, always pushing to be better than the day before.

I saw an innate desire in myself to build something as I got older. When I ventured out on my own for the first time as a fledgling entrepreneur, with a six-month-old, a wife, and a mortgage, I became acquainted with a fire within that wouldn't allow me to fail, regardless of what factors got in my way. In crafting my business development strategy for Causeway, all I did was tirelessly build relationships, one by one—flipping business cards, making phone calls, and sending follow-up emails, connecting with others by any means necessary, folks both known and those I'd never met. That led to more than three hundred meetings over coffee in the nine months prior to my founding Causeway Collaborative. Three hundred cups of coffee. Out of that, a business was born. One day at a time, one meeting at a time, one contact at a time.

But this year, I saw this idea highlighted in a way that I hadn't identified before. Yes, men are builders. This time, I relearned this from observing the approaches and practices of men who actually build things on a massive scale.

I had the opportunity to spend time around blue-collar men at a four-day speaking gig in the Midwest. I was facilitating a workshop on wellness and communication for fifty managers and leaders who work at a multibillion-dollar construction company, though most of us have never heard of it. Carpenters. Welders. Iron workers. Assemblers. These guys were men's men through and through.

They were tough—physically, mentally, and emotionally. Their conduct, values, behaviors, and consistency reeked of old-school Americana. They realized that work requires sacrifice. They understood that consistency is required in doing something of importance. In truth, given the business I run and the work I've done for so long, I forgot men like this existed. But they do—guys who came from Arkansas to work thirty-five days straight so they could enjoy ten days off to return to their families.

Guys who were third-generation union workers in the same trade as their fathers and grandfathers.

Guys who took up temporary residence on the Canadian border to work on an eight-billion-dollar project to rebuild one of America's great marvels of modern infrastructure that hadn't been repaired in nearly eighty years.

Guys who were willing to work twelve-hour days in frigid conditions to be able to make two to three times what they would make working at home.

Guys who had a mission to build generational wealth for their families. And prior to moving up north, they were driving one hundred miles one way to the jobsite in an effort to provide.

Yes, these men were builders, literally and metaphorically. They were committed to getting the job done. They were willing to do the hard work to see it through. They were patient, motivated by the very small gains they saw in front of them on a daily basis. And although many of these men struggled with the physical and emotional tolls of the burdens they inherited—loneliness, substance use, physical injury on their bodies, being away from their families, lack of relationships—these men saw their work as a small part of something bigger, something permanent, and something necessary for all of us.

They were building something bigger.

How do you build something?

To become a man, a young man must be willing to do the work required to build anything of substance. The journey from infant to man-child is paradoxically both long and instantaneous, as parents look back through recollection, memory, and images of when their shining star was but a child. Somewhere along that flash of road, the skinned knees and forgotten homework become bullying concerns, peer pressure, late-night parties, and pregnancy scares. This progression is nauseating for both a boy and his parents alike to consider. It happens faster than we care to admit.

As scary as it is for your son to be personally involved in a hard situation, it's also scarier for you, as his parent, to consider that he must learn to solve these situations without your help. A necessary and appropriate separation occurs between a young man and his parents, or his elders, wherein he becomes responsible for solving the problems he creates. Failing to do so fosters dependency, limits belief in one's own personal capacity, and creates anxiety that functions as a barrier to freedom. There are few better feelings for a man than a consistent belief in his ability to solve his own problems. There are also few things worse than him believing he cannot.

The majority of the work that we do with young men at Causeway actually stems from the over-involvement of their parents. The world we live in is a hyper-anxious place. We have access to a cascade of information related to how our sons are falling behind, how they are not keeping up with their peers, how their buddy is going to a top twenty-five school, and how jobs are hard to come by for men of any age. The byproduct of being overinformed on the prospective issues that men and young men face is that we (specifically parents) respond to situations impulsively and impatiently. As a result, parents can't refrain from stepping in.

As parents, we want to solve, we want to save, we want to be a hero for our kids. We become accustomed to the affirmation we receive when our kids are small and they look to us to rid the world of danger and provide reassurance that monsters don't exist under the bed. But as the problems associated with our sons get bigger, it becomes difficult for parents to rid themselves of the perceived burden to intercede.

What happens to a young man who isn't building a life of purpose? Who isn't building a vision for a life of his own design? What does he become?

When our kids have issues, it is far more difficult for us to allow them to figure things out for themselves than it has ever been. We're afraid they won't do a good job, or they'll fall behind. We're worried their buddy will do it better. And given our own impatience that stems from the pace of the world around us and the lifestyle we lead personally, we jump over them, pick up a hammer, and build the framework of their own life for them without their input.

In the fifteen years I've spent working with young men, I've seen parents exist largely unable to avoid this tendency. They've never had a harder time watching their kids make mistakes and giving them the room and the space to make it right.

It is important for young men to have structured, consistent, and orderly lives. In fact, developing those tendencies as men is fundamental to the process of building a life worth protecting.

Building order eliminates chaos

Through a functional lens, building something of our own design reestablishes order in our lives. See, it's not just about building something: It's about maintaining what you've built to ensure that it stands the test of time. I remember many years ago, a buddy who was our financial planner told me to "budget one percent of the purchase price of a home toward the cost of general upkeep and repairs." This included things like basic home maintenance, paint, interior and exterior renovations, and fixing things when they break. I never forgot that, and it made great sense to me at the time.

So what happens when things break down, or when we need to rebuild the broken infrastructure of our lives? What happens when things become so disordered in our world that we need to fully overhaul what once existed, gut it to the studs, and build something new in place of the old?

As a young man who was surrounded by chaos, my actions mirrored the world around me. My parents yelled at one another, communicated in ways that were problematic, made promises they couldn't keep, and were highly emotional. As those were the examples I was primarily exposed to, it was unsurprising that I embodied many of the same messy tendencies.

As a result, I began to personally develop an unstructured, volatile, aggressive, inconsistent lifestyle. It was hard for me to establish positive habits on a foundation of weak personality traits and flawed ways of being. Based upon my experience, I believe that only by purging some of the chaos from their lives and personally replacing those tendencies with different and more favorable ways of doing things can men engage in clean living and find a deeper sense of peace. Undoubtedly, a man has to do that work singlehandedly because if someone else steps in, that man himself will never be able to sustain the habit that someone else creates. In sum, I inherited the messiness of the life my parents built; thus, only I could clean that up for myself.

Since my foundation was unsteady, the habits I created as a young man made things even worse. I saw myself as a victim. I didn't think enough of myself at the time to believe I deserved to live a life of consistency and order. In many ways, if you asked the majority of the people who were around me at that time in my life, most would say I was, in fact, a victim, but unfortunately I used that mentality to rationalize dangerous, risky, illegal, and immoral behavior based upon the pain I experienced.

But now ...

As a coach and a mentor, it has become second nature for me to work alongside other men and help them clean up their messes and build their lives back, brick by brick. In many ways, the more unmanageable a situation is, the more comfortable I feel around it. As a young man, chaos felt familiar, conflict was my style of engagement, and aggressive and difficult interactions represented the customary way in which I engaged with people. That's why, when a guy whose life is out of control is in my line of sight, I always recognize his need to fully remodel his life.

When Nate showed up at Causeway after failing out of

college, I saw myself. He came back to Connecticut with his tail between his legs and a 0.6 GPA as the reward for his efforts during a semester of hard partying at college out West. To diagnose and effectively treat that situation, I applied a mentorship framework to our work because I had successfully navigated many of the same experiences he faced and stumbled through to the other side.

But before I get into Nate's story and how I supported him in reimagining his habits and remodeling his life, I'd like to dive into my own. This vignette demonstrates how to tear something down and rebuild it better, brick by brick.

I had a death wish

I remember, albeit blurrily, driving my sister, her best friend, and my buddy home at 2:30 a.m. after a night of partying, so drunk I had to pull over and throw up before I got back behind the wheel to continue toward my destination. Every weekend, I would go out and get messed up for forty-eight hours straight, drag myself home on Sunday at 8 p.m., and then drag my sorry self into school the following morning. That was how my junior and senior years of high school went.

During this time in my life, my parents were in the middle of a messy separation and eventually a messy divorce. My siblings and I were caught in the crossfire of lies, infidelity, denial, and incessant screaming matches.

So it's not surprising that I often didn't come home on Friday after school. Instead, I would head to practice and then bounce from couch to couch in pursuit of my next blackout, which I could usually find on both weekend nights. Showing up every Sunday still reeling from the weekend felt like a better alternative to my home life at the time.

I became far more than just your stereotypical meathead jock in high school. I had a death wish. I'd go out on the weekend and get aggressively drunk, far more than the people standing to my left and right did. It got to the point where I wasn't even interested in chasing girls on the weekends anymore; my sole purpose was to get as blasted as humanly possible, which was pretty much the only way I was able to cope with the mess going on in my life.

In fact, the chaos in my world manifested itself in terms of my head and my thinking. During the last semester of my senior year of high school, I was getting drunk every single day and never going to class. One might be asking at this point, "And you graduated? You're claiming you got drunk and skipped class every day for the last semester of senior year, and you were still able to graduate and walk with your class at commencement?" The answer, sad to say, is a resounding yes.

The consequence of not facing failure

At the time, I was glad to have skated through, undetected by school personnel and able to get to the finish line. Only now do I see what a grave injustice this was. Truthfully, I was significantly mentally ill, and just about every counselor in that school knew it. Everyone knew how much I was drinking and doing drugs; everyone knew what my weekend nonsense looked like, as evidenced by a few occasions where I came in with a black eye or a scraped-up face from a weekend skirmish. Sure, no one yet knew the precise mental health condition from which I was suffering, but I can tell you one thing as a clinician for many years: Had a professional intervened then, prior to my transition from high school into college, and forced me to address my mess at that time, that mess would have been far easier to clean up than it was three and a half years later. In truth, not failing in high school only accelerated the momentum of my freight train of chaos and made the failure that came later on down the line much more pronounced.

But even in spite of an ever-escalating mess that was building in scale and scope like an oncoming avalanche, I had done enough academically in the years prior that my circumstances didn't render me without options. By anyone's metrics of evaluation, I was a very good high school football player, certainly good enough to play in college, despite the ways in which my life was falling apart at the time.

Though I hobbled across the finish line in high school, I found myself at the very respectable Wesleyan University as a consolation prize. But my freshman year of college was basically an extension of the two-year nonstop high school party that precipitated it. Deplorable academic effort, minimal class attendance, and progressive use of alcohol, pot, and pills set the scene for the bottom to drop out the summer after my freshman year. That's when the cliff came.

The cliff

When I arrived home that summer, I became severely depressed. I distanced myself from friends. I quit my job. I isolated myself from the outside world, feeling ashamed of my depression and anxiety. I didn't understand mental health, didn't know how to make decisions that could help my situation and not exacerbate it. Worst of all, my family wasn't educated on these matters either, so they offered little in the way of guidance or support that could have proved useful in protecting me from me. I couldn't stop my descent into the abyss of my inner thoughts.

It got so bad that I was hospitalized for having thoughts of ending my life. I spent ten days as an inpatient at Yale Psychiatric Institute. I didn't accomplish much during my stay other than having my meds recalibrated, which allowed the medical team to observe my response to the new cocktail of pills they prescribed. When I was discharged in late July, the thought of not returning to college that fall scared me and escalated my anxiety, which stemmed largely from a deep-rooted fear of the unknown. What would I do if I took time off? How would people in my life respond? How would my future be impacted? Questions like this felt too messy and propelled me to rush my recovery.

A month later, I returned to Wesleyan, completely unready. I was paralyzed by escalating inner turmoil and a mind that was unwell. I didn't eat, wouldn't see friends, and couldn't even answer my phone. I locked myself in my room for three days and refused to answer my door when friends came to check on me. The crippling anxiety I was experiencing left me so ill-equipped to function that I was barely able to exist, let alone thrive as a student on a college campus.

After Public Safety kicked my door in and extracted me from my off-campus apartment, the only possible option was to take the semester off as a medical leave of absence.

Life as I had known it was over.

A long road

The journey from hospitalized, bipolar nineteen-year-old back to stable, sober, and more confident young man took me years to traverse. It was a gut-renovation job that was multidimensional in scope—one that no one could do for me.

Very real changes needed to happen, but they couldn't just be aspirational. I needed to make serious adjustments and practice them, repeat them, amend them, and make continued modifications as I went along. I made these tweaks part of my routine and part of how I operated on a daily basis. In fact, ironically, it was during my year of medical leave that I developed (without knowing it) the seedlings of the Causeway approach for a young man to get back to school. I began to clean up my own life and rebuild my lifestyle, brick by brick.

The overhaul in front of me then was both expansive and necessary. My academics were in shambles. I didn't have any structure to my life and my day. By this point, I was over sixty pounds heavier than my football weight in high school. In sum, the cleanup job was of epic proportion. With a lot of ground to cover, it felt like a good place to start was to fill my time with productive action. So, I did back then what we now recommend guys do in order to help them build confidence and develop new skills while away from college: I picked a place to start—and just got started. I signed up for two community college classes during my time off: a creative writing course, which would allow me to start writing about my experiences, and a statistics class, which would satisfy a prerequisite for my psychology major. I registered for these courses not because I was deeply invested in the work, but so that I could be accountable for moving my academic career forward. This coursework helped me regain some confidence around academic workflow and managing responsibilities as a student.

The Bs that I earned in both classes didn't speak volumes about my academic capacity, particularly comparing them with the curriculum I would face when I returned to take on four courses at Wesleyan. That said, they helped me sharpen my skills and manage my time, and they forced prosocial commitment and activity upon me at a time when I didn't feel like having any. See, part of treating depression is developing the capacity to do things when you don't feel like doing them. Community college in my two semesters off provided a valuable lesson in doing hard things despite my lack of personal investment in doing so.

The other essential component was work. I did another thing that we recommend our clients do in between semesters or when they take a year off. I got a job. It wasn't a great job. I worked at a deli around the corner from my house, a little hole in the wall called the Savory Café. I made sandwiches and coffee and worked the register. I had a forty-hour-per-week job for the entire year that I was off. This demonstrated to me a sustainable ability to consistently do something I didn't want to do. In the ability to grow grit in a young man or man, a requirement is sustained work in the face of adverse circumstances and often even a lack of motivation to do so. These steps were required in rebuilding my sense of self.

You gotta hate something to change it

I hated being away from school and learned how desperately I needed to get back there from my time off. I hated not being in the presence of my friends, who were having fun and doing outrageous things, which impressed upon me the need to get back in their presence. I hated being back in my parents' home, reimmersing myself in the chaos of their lives and their active disdain for each other. I hated the monotony of working a full-time job at a deli while not having the autonomy of a college kid, doing whatever I wanted, whenever I wanted.

Truth is, you gotta hate something to change it. I don't think anything changed for me prior to returning to Wesleyan after a one-year medical leave other than hating my situation while at home. It served as a foil to a life I wished to return to. I was so sick of sitting at home when my buddies were off doing fun things and going to college. I hated my circumstances and felt like any positive step was a step, so I was willing to take it, whatever forward movement I could find. I got humbled very hard. My humble pie lifestyle during that medical leave instilled a fire in me to build a life I could someday—someday far, far into the future—be proud of.

Where would it fit?

The big question for me when I went back to college was where and how football was going to fit into my very unmanageable life. I had always loved football, and for a while it was the biggest part of my life. When I was young, I was so skinny and underweight that my parents refused to let me put pads on until seventh grade. Although I only weighed 110 pounds, they recognized the need to get some experience playing organized ball before high school. I got on the field and fell in love. I was hooked.

For a few years while I was in high school, football may have kept me alive. Quite literally. The desire to play was the only form of accountability I had, internal or external. When I was at my worst—an angry, substance-using, confused seventeen-year-old man-boy—football was the only part of my life that made sense to me. When I was too angry to care about most things (my relationships, my academic performance, my physical self, and being a law-abiding member of society), football helped me organize myself and my mind.

It gave me an identity as someone who cared about a cause, who worked hard at something, and who took pride in being both part of a team and a leader on that team. At a time when I couldn't lead myself to make good decisions, it was far easier to be a good version of myself while leading others, particularly at something that mattered.

Given my love for football, I needed to sort that out first when I returned from my leave. I took the initiative on my first day back on campus and visited my coach's office, walking in confidently and looking him square in the eye as I shared the news of this incredibly difficult and life-changing decision. I told him everything: I needed to get my head right, I needed to do well in the classroom, and I needed to take better care of myself so I could come back next year and be ready to go.

The head coach, who was a terrible football coach and an even worse person, responded to me with a blank stare and an even colder retort: "Vinny, football is a four-year commitment. If you're not playing football this year, then you're not playing football here ever again."

"Okay," I responded. Then I shook his hand and walked out.

A little bit of my love for football died in that room that day. As a result, I needed to reinvent myself after circumstances beyond my control changed my universe.

I needed a new thing

By my junior year, as I motored along in the midst of innumerable changes, I had but one more significant adjustment to make. Whether I was ready or not, I had no choice but to overhaul my lifestyle.

Prior to my leave of absence, I had ballooned to around 270 pounds from years of alcohol use, poor eating, and an overall unhealthy lifestyle. My grades had been garbage; I had a 2.7 cumulative GPA without doing much work or exhibiting much care for my academics. My drinking and drug use had been consistent and escalating. I had also engaged in behavior that was escalating in danger and risk—fistfighting, drinking and driving, and putting myself in bad situations. I needed an overhaul.

In the single biggest decision I had made to date in terms of shaping the rest of my life's trajectory, I stopped drinking in 2003 at age twenty-two. I began to understand how important this was to help manage my mental health issues and to instill some semblance of equilibrium back into my life, and I was ready to make a switch. Sure, ceasing my alcohol consumption proved to be very difficult for a guy who drank very hard for five to six years prior; I'd built my foundational identity around substance use and hard partying. But ceasing my drinking helped me reprioritize my life and instill order into what was chaotic. I stopped staying up so late partying, so my sleep and overall health improved. I needed things to do, so I started exercising daily and lost a lot of weight. I got back in shape, started to feel good about myself, and bought some confidence back. And in the free time I bought back, I started (Ready for this?) going to class and doing my work for the first time in years. The impacts on my health, appearance, confidence, and academic performance were immediate and profound.

Although personal renovations didn't represent a complete transformation (a lot of aspects of myself still needed work), I experienced overwhelming progression. I ripped a 4.0 GPA for the last two semesters of my undergraduate degree, and for the first time since my sophomore year of high school—before alcohol and drugs took over my life—I was invested in my education. I began to feel some momentum stemming from buying back into caring about learning.

All the while, I was still working toward finishing my degree. On top of that, I was a teaching assistant in two psychology classes: One was The Psychology of Women, and the other was Abnormal Psychology. Despite not doing well prior to my academic pivot, I had a fantastic psychology professor, Dr. Russell, who later became my advisor. In my leadership of these classes, and through the work I was doing outside of that, I was shedding the label of a screwup and emerging as someone who could envision himself as a capable student. It had been a long time since I felt that way, but I remembered how good it felt.

Rebuilding my life pointed me toward my calling

Now that I was no longer one of the most outrageous guys on campus, nor was I raging nonstop with my buddies, time was something I possessed in great abundance. I coupled my new abundance of time with a desire to do more with it. I could get things done quickly and consistently. I also started helping others, volunteering to mentor young men in the inner city and picking up paid work as well, doing case management for a local nonprofit, trying to apply my learning in the classroom to see how it all fit. Not only did it fit, but my supervisors took notice. They said I was a natural at connecting with young men.

Once I started to clean up my lifestyle and rebuild my vision for my life, my world expanded. I went from someone who didn't have command of his life, his time, and his schedule to someone who possessed time, energy, and motivation and was looking for somewhere to put it. Slowly but steadily, I evolved into a young man who believed he had a calling—a strong desire to help other young men who suffered like me. I was motivated, for the first time in years, to do good in the world.

The Case of Nate

When Nate arrived at my office, he reminded me so much of myself that the pathway to his awakening felt eerily familiar. He came back to Connecticut with his tail between his legs and a 0.6 GPA as the reward for his efforts during a semester of hard partying at college out West. Having walked this path personally, I knew how to approach him, how to draw near to him, and how to slowly assist him in fixing his issues.

In high school, Nate was a fantastic athlete and community shining star who had hit the skids during his senior year. Nate was always concerned with what people thought of him, and it was historically difficult for him to say no to social situations of all shapes and sizes and their temptations. He was incredibly handsome, off-the-charts athletic, and highly competitive. In old photos, he looks like a young Justin Bieber, with blond highlights on full display but with an extra thirty pounds of muscle on his frame. Given those attributes, it was easy to see why he was the social epicenter of the town.

Nate didn't have a good sense of impulse control, loved to please others, and was concerned with his social standing, certainly above and beyond his investment in his academic and athletic pursuits. The truth was, he was just so talented at everything he did that it didn't really matter—best athlete, check; prettiest girlfriend, check; most handsome, check; could drink the most and do the most drugs, also check. His parents didn't feel like they had a choice but to send him away to a wilderness program to help get his life back on track.

Nate never forgave his folks for forcing him to miss his senior football season and that time with his friends. In spite of all that, he still received a full ride to college on a lacrosse scholarship. But after blowing out his knee the summer before his freshman year at Boston College in a freak men's pickup basketball league accident, he required season-ending knee surgery and had to forgo his scholarship award. He was destroyed.

Without a plan for the fall, he ended up at a huge school out in Washington. His parents felt the slower-paced and more balanced lifestyle coupled with the outdoors (which he deeply loved and built many hobbies around) would be a necessary foundation to a pivot in both identity and daily regimen. With the absence of lacrosse in his life, everyone involved knew Nate would require new ways of doing things, new interests to pursue, and other methods of spending his time.

Back then, only two states in the Union allowed people to buy, grow, and sell marijuana legally; attending a huge, sports-crazy Division I school in one of those states did nothing but expose Nate to a lifestyle of further substance abuse and escalating mental health symptoms. As a result, and based upon his personal similarities to me and my own situation, the circumstances of the case were ripe for him to be as solid a candidate as anybody to be one of the initial clients to come through Causeway. If anybody was going to be unwilling to do talk therapy but needed far more than just one hour per week on the couch, it was this kid.

So we hit the Go button

My work with Nate demonstrated the principle that talk therapy would never work with kids like this. Guys like Nate were far too oppositional for passive, patient, open-ended process work without a tangible result. Young me, like Nate, deeply valued his own time because of the social capital it carried; also, Nate saw therapy for what it was—largely fluff, unless implemented and executed extraordinarily well and with buy-in from the consumer.

Instead, my work with Nate demonstrated the efficacy of Futures Planning when applied to oppositional young men. He was an athlete, like many guys of this archetype (including myself), so my candor, tone, and the installation of structure provided a disciplined and regimented framework that males typically respond well to. He had done traditional therapy for years and hated it. Truthfully, he didn't need a stage to talk more about his problems. He had way too much energy and way too much free time to talk and not do.

So we hit the Go button on the Causeway Model, and it worked like a gem with this guy. The first thing we did was square him up (provide direct commentary on what needed to be done and put forth a basic and clear path forward) and get him a job. My only criteria were that the job was structured and full time—in many ways, the worse the job, the better in this situation. I correctly intuited that Nate would benefit from some humble pie to cut his larger-than-life ego down to size.

After a few weeks, our process flowed rather seamlessly from initial goal-setting to résumé development, cover letter design, and interview prep. Almost immediately, as a result of our efforts, Nate found himself doing construction thirty-five hours per week, making more money than was necessary for him to independently fund living on his own. The esteem that came from him being able to support himself, absent assistance from his very wealthy parents, was amazing. For the first time in his life, his successes were entirely his own. He was able to engage in a task, follow through to completion, and achieve a result—all of his own doing. He immediately felt the fulfillment that came with that process. Sure, the bar was lower than before, now that he was a college dropout with no scholarship doing a tour of duty at community college. But in his eyes and in mine, his current plan was more than sufficient for now.

Slow and steady, but moving forward

We were both comfortable with moving slowly and making steady upward progress. But there were some clear, uniform expectations we shared. There was no room in our codesigned framework for doing less. I asserted that Nate needed to be intentional about adding positive and structured activity to his life, not subtracting. He agreed.

Nate was working construction for thirty-five to forty hours per week. His work was hands-on, so the job itself functioned in a productive fashion to tire him out, which helped him get to bed earlier, and he became an early riser. Old Nate could have never imagined there would be a world where he was in the shower at 4:45 a.m., getting ready for his day. That became the norm. Truth is, the biggest secret here is that in getting up so early and occupying himself in those ways, Nate didn't have time or room to engage in the shenanigans that had become a mainstay of his old life.

He also started liking what he saw in himself physically. He lost some of the beer weight he had put on at school and got back under his former playing weight for lacrosse. He was motivated by those physical gains to start going to the gym after work each day. Two days became four and five days per week pretty quickly, and alongside a nice golden-bronze tan that came from taking his shirt off at work every day, Nate became more confident in himself, and his depressive inclination started lifting. He began drinking less and not partying quite as hard on the weekends. Granted, it was challenging for him to ignore the social influences that pulled at him now that he was back home for the summer after freshman year.

We hunkered down and further committed ourselves to our primary ingredient in this recipe all along: Add more good things to his life, under any and all circumstances. Come fall, we registered him for one community college course on top of his forty-hour-per-week construction job. The next semester, it was two courses. Unbelievably, he earned Bs in all three of his classes with very little work put in outside of large-scale assignments. Despite being pleased with his progress, with the results representing pure magnificence when stacked alongside his 0.6 GPA from his time in Washington, ironically Nate was only beginning to scratch the surface of his capabilities as a student.

The gasoline in this case came in the form of Nate's decision to go back to college full time. Again, he had never succeeded academically, so he never identified himself as someone who was truly capable. This belief set was only affirmed and solidified by his dumpster fire of an academic performance while in Washington.

Unfinished business

We decided to apply to a state school in New York, where Nate was able to walk on and try his hand at lacrosse one more time. This gave him the opportunity to address some unfinished business. Not only did he walk on to the team, but he was able to start almost immediately as a junior, become a captain as a senior, win All-League honors his final year, and have a fantastic time while doing so.

Lacrosse for Nate was an extraordinary experience and a phenomenal way for him to punctuate his college career. The best part is that as a freshman standing in the wake of the wreckage of his first year of school in Washington, what Nate accomplished by the end of college would have been viewed by most everyone as virtually impossible.

Like his teacher and coach, Nate achieved a 4.0 GPA for the last two years of school. Sure, he was out and about, and, yes, he was partying and running around like a wild man socially, but he was locked in and focused in the classroom and had direction that had sorely evaded him prior. Nate even decided he wanted to go into the mental health field so he could work with guys who had backgrounds like his.

It's got to be personal

Once Nate received support that he valued, put the structure and framework of his life back in order, and had enough productive activities on his calendar to fill his time in meaningful ways, amazing things happened. With support, relationships, and the right type of help, Nate was equipped with the tools that allowed him to build his life, brick by brick. Nate gut-renovated his life personally, which is why the changes stuck and have been sustained.

A very personal business

Building things brick by brick eventually equipped me with the knowledge to help guys like Nate rebuild a different kind of life. At Causeway, alongside our guys, we aren't afraid to rebuild a mess, and we aren't afraid to clean it up along the way. We model for young men a bygone way of doing things: to do a hard thing, to continue trying it until you improve and eventually succeed, and then move toward the next hard thing on your way to something beautiful of your own design. Remodeling my own life, personally, is why the changes stuck and have been sustained for me, and it's why I can strategize and model those kinds of adjustments so effectively for someone else.

In sum, the life-designing business is a very personal one. You can't depend on anyone to do it for you, nor should you. Your parents fixing your life will rob you of the opportunity to grow and change, to learn and develop valuable skills, and to become a different and better version of yourself. Relying on them fosters dependency and limits potential.

But your life also can't be remodeled for you by your therapist. I say this as a licensed therapist for over a dozen years, by the way. Doing individual therapy with a disengaged nineteen-year-old into infinity, with no advice, coaching, deliverables, or tangibles—with no exposure, correction, and guidance—is like sending a client into the African savanna solo to get eaten by a lion. That man-boy is not going to be able to course correct or have perspective about the inputs around him, around the problems that could befall him. How could he? He's never seen them before. He lacks the experience to understand the scope of the choices around him, or even worse, the poor lad will spin his wheels relentlessly without action, while his parents (who are undoubtedly paying the bill) are stroking checks for $250 per session per week without end. Nate's parents had tried this approach for years, and it was the lack of direction, support, and advice, given his lack of experience in the world, that made it such a fruitless endeavor. It wasn't until he took matters into his own hands that things were rebuilt, remodeled, and fixed—and stayed that way.

So take it personally, men, and build it back, brick by brick. Let it take as long as it has to. Be persistent and don't give up, no matter how arduous the journey. And parents, take your son's development personally, too. Let him get messy and fix things up himself. It is important for young men to make mistakes so they can learn. Failure builds character and helps promote esteem and self-efficacy. Getting things wrong is essential for building skills through experiential learning about how to get them right—to try and fail, and fail small, so that failure in larger and more complex ways can be circumnavigated. Building things back brick by brick gives a young man the opportunity to fix things up for themselves. These reps are essential for learning, improving, and taking forward steps in their own growth and development.

TIPS FOR GUYS

There is no problem that is too big to solve, brick by brick. It may take more time or more effort than initially imagined, but there is nothing that is impossible to repair through time, sustained effort, and commitment. Nothing.

Rebuilding things, brick by brick, teaches valuable lessons. Mistakes show us what not to do and help us adjust for the future.

Our mess can become our gift. By learning from and fixing our mistakes, we gain the power to guide others away from the same pitfalls. Turning struggle into purpose is a choice—and a gift.

TIPS FOR PARENTS

Let your son handle his own messes. Though it's hard to watch, struggling and failing on his own builds resilience and independence. It's essential for him to rebuild things, brick by brick.

Let your son face the consequences of his actions. Cleaning up after him steals valuable lessons that only personal experience can teach.

Avoid problem-solving for your son, skipping steps, or rebuilding things on his behalf. Doing so can signal doubt in his ability, which can hurt more than help.

LESSON 2

Name It to Tame It

REGARDLESS of the code of the Old West and your thoughts about the absence of rules in that landscape, most people admire cowboys. Historically speaking, they are icons for conventional male notions of masculinity: unshaven, stoic, strong, cool-headed, and blue-collar in their approach. Cowboys do hard things; they are required to be brave at all times, and even in the face of their own fear, cowboys prioritize doing what's necessary over what is in their best interests. Sometimes cowboys win—think shooting down a vigilante bad guy in the town square in the climax of the film—but sometimes they lose, falling victim to a bank robbery where the bad guy gets away with massive bags of gold in both hands. Either way, regardless of the circumstances and the outcome, cowboys universally share one common trait: Under no circumstances does a cowboy give up, especially when things get hard or dangerous.

When most boys consider conventional notions of manhood and masculinity, they think of a "Marlboro Man," cowboy-esque archetype. High value is placed upon ideals of toughness, stick-to-itiveness, stoicism, and protecting others (even at the expense of oneself). Thus, as we grow up and become young men and then men, there is often a narrow-mindedness around the expectations of how we, as young men, should behave. This is certainly true in the realm of feelings, where there's a universal answer for the question of what we should feel as young men growing up in this world: nothing.

This inability to communicate emotion also underscores the realm of physical pain. How often, in film, movies, TV, and literature does a cowboy or a superhero get injured, or shot, and continue to move forward undeterred? Maybe the hero ties a piece of cloth around his wound and keeps walking forward? Or maybe he rubs some dirt on his scraped knee if he's less experienced, and his wound is smaller in scope? When a man doesn't name it, he keeps moving forward in his life, plagued by his wound, but unable to treat the root cause, pretending instead that it doesn't exist.

More accurately, it's not precisely that we should feel nothing as men but more so that whatever we feel, we shouldn't respond to. When you fall off your bike and skin your knee as a kid, every dad (myself included) wants his boy to pop up, dust off his hands and knees, affirm that he's fine, march himself over to his bike, and pick up where he left off (unless his arm is hanging from a thread of connective tissue, of course). When a boy is sad, a father expects his son to articulate what he is upset about but not allow the circumstance to affect him emotionally (mothers often expect this too). The message from a very young age is to communicate effectively but exhibit only consistency and stability emotionally. Anything else is seen by parents as abnormal.

As a society, we are very comfortable with seeing our daughters, girls, and young women express themselves emotionally. Even when girls are extremely emotional, we rationalize their intense displays of emotion and accept them with a degree of comfort and acceptance. The same is not true for men. When men become ashamed, discouraged, indecisive, or terrified, we don't know how to receive their outpourings of affect, certainly not with the same degree of comfort we can readily achieve with their female counterparts.

The truth

It's easy to see why as men and young men we're so resistant to therapy and to receiving help in general. In the eyes of men across our broader society, if we as men seek help, we're weak and needy, and it implies that we are incapable of independently solving our own problems or supporting ourselves through our own challenges. It is the opposite of being tough, the opposite of being a cowboy, the opposite of falling off your bike and getting back on immediately. It is both hardwired in men and instructed by society to fix a problem when it presents itself, not sit on your heels and patiently explore the root causes while a professional probes into your personal affairs and psyche—the last two places that most any man wants any stranger. By the way, the therapeutic relationship necessitates by its ethical guidelines that the professional remains a stranger by role definition, that he or she asks all the questions while you deliver all the answers, pouring your guts out on the coffee table, session after session, week after week, without him or her sharing any modicum of personal information whatsoever in return. This, again, is another reason why I don't think therapy alone works for young men, and why I've worked for my entire life to develop something that does.

But the truth is, men need to heal too. Our wounds hurt. When we are hurt and wounded, we need to treat the injury and recover. Just grinning and bearing it is insufficient. It deprives us as men of the ability to become more in touch with our emotions and develop emotional fluency, and it also deprives us of knowledge of self. In order for us to move toward self-discovery in the process of building personal insight, we need to identify our issues and challenges in order to develop a plan of action to overcome them. We need to name it to tame it.

As a young man, I became afflicted with both severe mental health issues and severe addictive tendencies. Those challenges initially invoked fear in me that I was not only "less than" when compared to other men, but that those conditions were permanent. As a result of the staying power of those labels, I believed I was relegated to a life and a set of outcomes that were automatically going to be less than: less than my peers, less than what my own ceiling would have been, and less than the expectations others had established for me.

The truth was, although I couldn't see it at the time, my labels and my willingness to accept them were the answer, the antidote, and the prescription. By doing the things that were proven to provide relief, by incorporating the behaviors that provided structure and support, and by accepting the help from people who had knowledge of the subject, I was able to boost my own resilience, armor myself against threat, and more effectively manage my physical, mental, and emotional health. Once I was willing to call out my issues by name, I began the process of taming the beasts I faced.

I was in no way ready

In the years since my own journey with mental health began, I've tried to shepherd other men and young men through navigating their own experiences of healing. Often this involves a process of self-discovery that allows a young man freedom of choice, freedom to identify a vision, learning the skills to execute a plan, developing a sense of how he thinks and feels about his progress along the way, and receiving the support of his parents in doing so. Under these ideal circumstances, young men can learn, evolve, and thrive.

But as a young man, my circumstances were far from ideal. During my parents' divorce, it seemed everything they said was a lie. There was a tremendous amount of personal identity stuff that came up for me as a result of that realization. There was a profound lack of trust and clarity. This confusion centered largely around the absence of a sense of order in the world. As a young man, when you live in a world of mixed signals and are told so many overt lies, it's hard to know which way is up or down.

Through therapy, reflection, and deep personal work over the last twenty-plus years, I found the roots of many of my deepest issues in that season of my life, issues that plagued me into adulthood. As I bore witness to my mother berating my father, eviscerating him for his poor decision-making, recklessness, and selfishness, I became overwhelmingly defensive and even self-righteous in my positions about most matters. I now understand this was an overcorrection, a coping mechanism. This led to me feeling hypersensitive to criticism for much of my adult life. It took years in therapy and hard work to develop these personal insights to correct the emotional challenges that bore roots in my later teens.

Underneath, I was also very insecure. A major part of me saw myself as both broken and undesirable, fully incapable of receiving love. As I observed my father being accused of being a gay man by my mother, as he denied those allegations while he worked through his process of coming out, as my mother spewed venom about his lying to cover it up, I questioned, well, everything: Who can I trust? How can I love these people? They're hurting us so much, and they are so messy themselves. Who am I as a young man in the world if my own adult male role model can't make sense of who he is? What does it say about me if my own mother is so filled with venom, rage, and hate? These guys are my parents, so aren't those vile elements of their story an inevitable part of me, too? And why do I keep trying to destroy myself? More importantly, why can't I stop? I didn't have the language at the time to articulate these considerations. I was a locomotive that had gone far, far off the rails.

I don't remember much from my first hospitalization, but I do remember the group therapy component, seeing and hearing from individuals who had been hospitalized four, eight, even upward of ten times. Men of color, women of color, young girls, old men, old women. The diversity of the census on the unit demonstrated to me what I already knew but had never internalized: Mental health knows no restrictions in terms of who it impacts and how severely it does so.

People shared their heart-wrenching stories of how their lives had been ripped apart by their issues, how substance use plagued them for decades, how their jobs wouldn't be waiting for them when they came out of the hospital, and even in some cases how their hospitalization was court-mandated because of issues with the law.

You would imagine that this type of exposure, this window into what my fate could look like if I didn't make massive overtures to turn my life around, would serve as an incredible motivating factor for me to transform my existence. Unfortunately, at that time, my depressive inclination was so deeply rooted and overwhelming that I still couldn't develop any meaningful traction in moving toward feeling better.

In truth, back then, no one knew the severity of how I felt except me. I knew how much I hated myself and hated my life. I was in no way ready to accept my label as a bipolar alcoholic, both facets of that description being permanent in scope. Instead, I saw this description as evidence of the magnitude of my own brokenness.

Fits and starts

By the time I came to a reasonable understanding of myself in college, I hated who I was. I saw myself as barely recognizable. In truth, I detested my conduct, but I wasn't honest enough or brave enough to say that out loud. The truth was, all my substance-using, promiscuous hard partying, and late-night unhealthy nonsense only made me feel empty and awful about myself. Yet it was the only way I knew how to socialize. When you go to college, and you're a young man, aren't you supposed to get drunk and chase girls? Isn't that what you do? Particularly as a meathead football player?

Thus, my acceptance of my diagnosis was a process that moved forward in fits and starts. My worldview was so narrow that I didn't really see any other options. At that time, I had some temporary moments of clarity. I would take the blinders off for a little while, but I got really depressed about what I saw when I looked around. These observations occurred in ways that both scared me and confused me. This is one of the reasons that guys struggle to be honest with themselves in accepting the scope of their situations: Once they see the work required to fix the situation and understand what they need to do and for how long, they become afraid. So they avoid being accountable to the steps they need to take.

I saw myself as a follower, a substance user who lacked meaningful relationships. I was disgusted by my promiscuity, the ways I had casual sexual relationships without meaning and purpose. I was hardened by the fact that football was no longer a part of who I was, but more powerfully, that I was responsible for losing it because I never prioritized it. I hated these insights I had recently gained. But ironically, when I went back to college, I put the mask back on and kept going. It was so much easier than being honest with myself about my place in the world, who I was, and who I had become.

As a result, I continued to flounder. Because of my inability to name my issues, they persisted. As I demonstrated a lack of ability to be brave and accept the scope of my challenges by name, I was unwilling to take the steps necessary to correct them. The partying continued. The substance use persisted. The academic disengagement lingered. I continued to sleepwalk through the malaise of my previous college existence even after my medical leave.

It was only when I accepted my diagnosis as a bipolar young man that I could begin to take the steps to treat the symptoms of the problem. First, I needed to come to peace with my condition being both chronic and lifelong. It was something that I debated the validity of for a while. Initially, I felt I was flawed in so many ways, and so significantly, that it was hard to acknowledge. I was scared of what people would think of me if they were aware of my mental illness. I was personally afraid of future bouts of both depression and mania taking hold of my life again. I was fearful of my inability to manage my symptoms for the rest of my life, knowing the volume of work that would be required to do so.

Lack of acceptance is common for men who suffer from severe mental illness. Unlike a cowboy, I had to acknowledge that my severe mental illness made me both limited and fallible. I required a certain amount of regular and consistent sleep. Substance use, especially to the degree that I was engaging previously, would put me at higher risk for future episodes of both depression and mania. I needed to eat well and exercise regularly to help manage the inconsistency of my mood. Most importantly, I needed to accept that I had to take medication every day for the rest of my life. The side effects of these very same meds were profound, so much so that when I started my mood stabilizer while I was in the hospital, I gained nearly fifty pounds over a period of three months. Obviously, I was resistant to taking pills as a result because as a formerly vain, fit, and athletic guy, my prescription rendered me overweight, less confident, and looking like a far less attractive version of myself.

After about two years of vacillation and inconsistency in

my acceptance, I came to terms with both of my diagnoses as a bipolar alcoholic. From there, I understood what I needed to do and the steps I needed to take. The drinking, given its frequency and the risks it presented, needed to be the first domino to tip. At the time, the single biggest factor impeding my progress in life was casting aside my use of substances. My relationships with my girlfriend and friends were becoming too problematic, and my behavior was out of control. Once I stopped drinking at the age of twenty-two, I began to see an immediate and permanent improvement in my mental health, relationships, and overall sense of wellness. From there, I committed myself to getting back in shape, and over about six months, I dropped thirty pounds. I was back in the gym six days a week. But I also needed to translate my momentum to the classroom. I knew that if I wanted to increase my chances of getting a job after college, I needed to improve my grades. I started going to class, taking notes, and taking my performance seriously. I became more invested in my relationships, following through on my commitments. I exerted more time and energy into my friendships, not focusing specifically on activities where I was using drugs and alcohol, but spending more time in one-on-one frameworks and more meaningful conversations, and doing things that served those with whom I was in a relationship. I was also slowly becoming a healthier, more balanced version of myself, finding more motivation to seek personal interests and even to prioritize downtime and rest.

For me, naming and addressing my issues, specifically my alcoholism and mood disorder, gave me a clear path that I needed to traverse. More importantly, knowing what steps to take to treat my issues made it infinitely easier for me to make and sustain progress.

The same was true of Jacob. He came to me hostile and broken. He was confused and afraid of the newly applied diagnostic label he faced and the corresponding implications it would bear on both his life and his future. Initially, the scope of the work we could even attempt to do was highly limited because of his resistance to understanding who he was and all that came along with it. But since he shifted his position on his willingness to learn about himself, now accepting his label and all of its corresponding implications, Jacob is charting a course for a future that he previously did not think possible. I am fortunate enough to have hung in there long enough to still be standing beside him.

The Case of Jacob

JACOB was tall and slim. He kept his head shaved tight, not quite to the skin but about as short as you could bring it down with a clipper. Often, he was dressed in monochromatic attire, wearing powder-blue T-shirts with jeans, or black V-neck tees with faded black pants. Fashion evaded him, for sure. Loquaciousness did not. Jacob could go on and on and on, so long as he was spinning yarn on something he enjoyed talking about. Yes, those subjects most certainly lacked breadth, which frustrated his parents immensely.

Jacob's complexion was naturally dark, but it had grown pale gray through a lack of exposure to sun because he rarely went outside. Jacob was very self-conscious around girls, but as his parents often said, he had the looks in the family. He had kind, crystal blue eyes, but they didn't always show up that way; he often stared blankly and coldly as he engaged in conversation. His jaw was sharply square, showing off his naturally lean, slender physique. Had Jacob been equipped with a different demeanor and inclination, he could have done well in initiating relationships with women at school.

Jacob's family

Jacob's father, who paved his own way in business, carried his own father's work ethic like the badge of honor that it was. Jacob's dad had immense pride in his own father: a man who came with nothing, gave all he had every day of his life, and rewarded his children with opportunities he never knew existed as a young man, let alone imagined. Jacob's grandfather pledged that his own children would be able to have the opportunity to do anything they wanted to with their lives, based upon his efforts and sacrifice. Jacob's father took that opportunity seriously. He made good on it.

It was important for Jacob's grandfather to ensure that his kids didn't work in the family business. Instead, they would go to college fully funded and hopefully be educated beyond that. With his at bat, Jacob's dad put one in the bleachers, hitting a full-blown grand slam. He went to an Ivy League university—the very same one his son later attended. He parlayed a degree in engineering into a job on Wall Street some thirty years ago. He ascended there quickly and moved into venture capital, then private equity, always making a jump, always seeking the next opportunity. Calculated move after calculated move led to the accumulation of exponential wealth. With every transition, Dad accrued more contacts, more favors, more influence. Finance turned into computers, then the cloud, then alternative energy, and now artificial intelligence. Dad, now fifty-three, finds himself semiretired, sitting on three or four boards of major Fortune 500 companies, with more money than he can count. All because Jacob's grandfather was a cowboy, doing what was required, every day, without ever complaining.

Jacob's place

Growing up, when Jacob would ask his father for an Xbox or a PS4 or a moped, he would be met with immediate resistance. Instead, Jacob was redirected to intellectual pursuits: reading, music, and the arts. Jacob often spent time at friends' homes—some of which had indoor basketball courts, in-home movie theaters, and indoor swimming pools. For Jacob, the primacy of money came from competing in the most elite of social stratospheres, all while his parents were attempting to embody the principles of fiscal responsibility and good stewardship. The roots of the issues between Jacob and his father found footing in the persistent stream of "No" that Jacob received to requests made as a young boy.

Mom was far more forgiving and kind. She was blond, bubbly, effervescent, and physically fit. Her face showed the age from years spent in corporate during her early career prior to her husband's extensive success. Eventually, she decided it no longer made sense to work a full-time job. She turned to volunteering and leadership roles in nonprofit work, and her life consisted largely of lunch dates, tennis matches, training sessions, and service initiatives. She and her son got along reasonably well—but only when no one else was around to intercede. Otherwise, she was relegated to the role of peacekeeper, as Dad often accelerated his son's resistance.

Being different

Jacob recognized that he was different, but he didn't quite understand how and why. He once told me he didn't carry the same "masculine energy" as other boys his age. He went to an elite private school from kindergarten through twelfth grade, and he was quick to identify that the other boys there were more popular, more athletic, and better looking than he. Jacob saw himself as less than, and when he was picked on, he resolved to bear the abuse, feeling like it was a better alternative to getting beat up by the other kids, which happened on the only two times he did attempt to verbally stand up for himself. For Jacob, it was easier to be anonymous, passive, and virtually unknown than it was to face scrutiny and abuse.

As I mentioned, Jacob got into the very same Ivy League college his father had attended, where Dad became a large benefactor to the university. Jacob saw college, particularly one as prestigious as this school, as his great equalizer. He had been told his whole life this narrative of success: Study hard, work your ass off, go the extra mile, get into a great school, and doors will open onto you. The elite private all-boys day school he'd attended for twelve years fueled this belief set, and he clung to it hook, line, and sinker.

His vision for the world away at school was one where he would meet droves of young men (and young women, for the first time) who were just like him and who shared common interests. These preconceptions were grounded in some significant truths and had been shared and repeated to him year after year after year. He embraced college as his real chance to build the kind of version of himself that he had always been promised he'd become.

... Until he didn't

Jacob's freshman year was largely uneventful. He achieved Bs and Cs, but the work was harder than he expected. Moreover, it was challenging for him to manage his free time and spend it in meaningful ways that promoted relationship. In fact, after being rejected in a couple of social attempts to put himself out there and earnestly try to make friends, he largely sequestered himself in his room, playing video games and reading articles on the computer. Sophomore year, an off-color comment late one night on social media made him a social pariah of sorts. Although it's unclear how damaging that comment actually was versus how much people's perceptions lived in Jacob's mind, it didn't really matter.

Jacob was not only wounded but also paranoid about what others thought of him. He was isolated. He was friendless. He was alone. And so it was, by the end of his first semester of sophomore year, Jacob found himself at home on medical leave, significantly depressed and faced with the repercussions of withdrawing from two classes, which he did to avoid taking Fs in classes that he'd stopped attending.

Needless to say, when I started my work with Jacob, he was very angry. In fact, one of the first things that this client told me on the phone (after asking me if I had kids) was that he wished physical harm upon them and hoped they would struggle like he knew I had struggled in my own past. Given my temper, love for my children, and genuine disdain for anyone who talks trash to me in any way, shape, or form, my countertransference was raging, as I'm sure you can imagine. It was essential for me to ground myself in the issue at hand, remain calm, and focus on the scope of both his challenges and his pain.

The issue at hand

Truth was, Jacob had found out that very same week that he was on the autism spectrum. He was twenty-one years old, on medical leave from an Ivy League school for issues that were beyond the scope of his and his family's understanding. His parents were extremely intelligent, extremely successful, and even more well connected. How could they not know? If they did know, how could they not share it with him? And for him, what did this label mean? What did it convey about who he was as a person and what his life would look like going forward?

The work with Jacob was challenging. He was angry and highly isolated with absolutely zero peer-based interaction whatsoever. According to him, women had, and I quote, "way too many privileges and don't deserve equal pay or equal rights." This was going to be interesting. Additionally, Jacob believed his Ivy League college was not a good fit because it was "overrun with liberal minorities who made it so that kids like me didn't have opportunities." It was easy to see why Jacob was so unlikable. And it was also easy to see what that off-color comment on social media might have sounded like to the students who viewed it. Frankly, like many others, most of me couldn't stand this kid ... until I saw the roots of his pain.

Jacob had a father he would never be able to match in intelligence and achievement and a mother who was kind and compassionate but somewhat coddling in her approach, conveying an implicit belief that he was unable. This illustrated what was certainly at least mild relational discord between Jacob's parents, as a strong incongruence existed between Dad's tough love approach and Mom's softer, gentler, more consistent relational emphasis.

The real jam-up

The real jam-up for Jacob was the spectrum diagnosis. I sent him out for a neuropsychological assessment to corroborate the label. This one was tough, as there were shades of a few different prospective symptom clusters: Borderline Personality Disorder, PTSD, a mood disorder, Oppositional Defiant Disorder, depression, and/or anxiety. Each of these unique conditions has a continuum of severity, so any one of them was a possibility to some degree.

But the diagnosis of Autism Spectrum Disorder tied it all together. It explained his rigidity and his unwillingness to hear feedback and entertain new ways of doing things. It explained his challenges in integrating socially and connecting with people on campus. It illuminated why social nuance evaded Jacob, making it impossible to deeply understand humor, sarcasm, and implicit messaging. But most of all, it allowed his team to see that he was limited in his flexibility and his ability to make change, which explained why the medical leave was so jarring in the first place.

For Jacob's entire life, he was told that college was the key to success. He studied hard, got into an amazing school, never got in trouble, and played by the rules. So it's unsurprising, given that he's also on the spectrum, that when that plan went belly-up, it absolutely crushed him. Most typical students struggle with this kind of rejection, failure, and deviation from plan. For Jacob, it was more than he could bear. This label made him, by his own admission, "feel like a cripple." He resisted the diagnosis. "I'm not a cripple," he declared, "and I refuse to acknowledge this BS." If I wanted to connect with Jacob and help him reexamine his circumstances, I would have to find another way.

Just stay in it

Jacob came to me with his malicious, intentionally shocking statements within the first two weeks of our work. He was broken, wounded, and looking to sever relationships with anyone and everyone who was trying to help him or shift his perspective in any way. He later admitted he was just trying to say the most provocative and hurtful things that he could as a result of his pain and confusion. Based upon his presentation, it was obvious my work was cut out for me, but in no way would I take his bait and recuse myself from the assignment at hand.

I did what I always do in these situations: Stay in it. Just stay in it. Evade any attempts by the client to self-sabotage or cause me to tap out on the situation. I stayed connected, never missing an appointment and holding him to the same standard. I leaned in. I got to know him, listened to his interests, and learned what his goals were. I was patient. I remained non-judgmental, even when his remarks bordered on the intolerable.

Like most guys on the spectrum, Jacob had no problem delving into his interests for long periods of time, embarking on unbroken explanations about crypto, US history and the nation's impending demise, the uselessness of women, and the primacy of money in all matters of life. In other words, not exactly the sort of late-night conversation threads likely to help him build bonds with his peers. For now, though, Jacob just needed an audience, and I served his needs well. I never judged him; I opposed him when appropriate, but always in a respectful and calm manner that never revealed my distaste for his views. Over time, I earned his trust. In doing so, I gained, in his eyes, the credibility to very occasionally push up against his ideas and offer suggestions in an effort to promote some modicum of change. I did this patiently over the course of our work, with escalating measures of both firmness and challenge as time passed.

Without acceptance, we were limited

I'm still unclear whether Jacob's parents knew he was on the spectrum prior to our work beginning. Their initial assertion was a resounding no, which I guess was possible, but it certainly didn't coincide with their intuition, intellect, aggressiveness, and desire to problem-solve. If they did know, they certainly were unwilling to share it, likely feeling as if Jacob's awareness of being different would have profound and longstanding consequences.

They had hoped receiving this label would provide important insights about why his time at school was unsuccessful and how he could successfully transition back. Jacob was also burned by the fact that the narrative of the ideal life he was seeking didn't work out as he was told it would: Go to school. Do your best. Work hard. Don't screw up. This, in Jacob's mind, meant success was a guarantee. Instead, for him, loneliness and hardship prevailed.

Jacob and I did what we could. Without accepting his diagnosis, we were limited in our options to cover effective ground. We practiced relationship, shared reciprocal and appropriate dialogue, and worked to foster socialization in our work in session, creating plans for prosocial engagement in his weeks outside of session. We also incorporated his parents into the treatment plan as surrogates, functioning as a valuable social interface in the world, absent real companions for Jacob. His parents did the best they could to fill the void that other social interfaces might have afforded under different circumstances. The contrived social interface that his parents and I provided allowed us to make some progress, treating symptoms of the problem and allowing for some change to begin.

Out of nowhere ...

Recently, seemingly out of nowhere, Jacob sent me the following text: "Hey, just some prep for tomorrow, if you don't mind. Want to talk about my diagnosis. What it means for my wellness, and others. Dealing with it, integration, etc. Don't know if there's materials or the like I can read up on before we talk about stuff like this. Thx."

What? Was he finally ready to name it?

Turns out that Jacob got a job at a doctor's office. His father had struck up a conversation with the doctor there; the two of them had been friendly while Jacob's dad had been under her care. She also had a son at home from college who was in a similar situation as Jacob. To Jacob, this meant he wasn't alone. He wasn't the only one who was in his situation and who had these struggles. With that, he began to see the situation with different eyes. When his dad told the doctor Jacob was looking for work, she was more than happy to hire him.

Once Jacob was given the opportunity, his parents offered to help him in whatever additional ways he needed. But recognizing an opportunity, Jacob saw this situation as something unique and different. It served as the motivation for him to reexamine whether the diagnostic label he had received had been a factor in some of the challenges he had faced prior. Additionally, he thought a better understanding of that label might help him be more successful in this coming role, using it as rehearsal for what might come down the line, in a brighter version of his future. A future he had previously thought was lost.

Jacob's life started to improve. He worked at the doctor's office twenty-four hours per week and secured an internship for the following summer. He and his mother began working out together in the mornings, providing a chance for him to spend some time with her, engage in a fitness routine, and accomplish something hard each day. Although Jacob and Dad's relationship remained tense, they got along better and talked more consistently without conflict. They even made plans to go away for a weekend and do some projects on the family's summer house.

"Jacob," I said in our last session, "you sound awesome. Are you doing anything differently this week?"

"I'm just trying to be more positive," he said. "I'm not even close to truly being a positive person, but I'm consistently trying hard. I think that no matter what, having a good attitude will benefit me no matter what I do in life. I'm just trying to control the things that I can control."

Now that's a far cry from wishing harm on my offspring. I'll chalk that one up in the win column.

Accepting limitations

Like his therapist, Jacob made sustainable progress when he accepted the scope of his limitations. In many ways, his personal limits not only provided clarity, but they helped him reorder his priorities as well as lean into his areas of strength and away from his places of weakness. The next step in our work was to explore the process of exposure therapy, naming and operationally defining his levels of anxiety when facing certain specific stimuli. From there, we planned to map the appropriate intervention to address and extinguish his anxiety in each circumstance. All of this work, as well as the new commitments Jacob took on, came from an acceptance of his diagnostic label and the steps he was willing to take thereafter.

Avoiding our labels and the names associated with them allows men to avoid hard conversations. We don't have to acknowledge troubles in our marriages. We don't have to identify when we are vulnerable and have a health concern or are struggling with performance issues. We don't have to acknowledge when we have learning disabilities or conditions like ADHD that make it difficult for us to pay attention and concentrate. We don't have to examine our behaviors—like my alcohol use when I was an active alcoholic, which was causing significant issues in my relationships at the time.

But as men and young men, it's not solely about the labels that are applied and the behaviors they highlight; it's about the emotions connected to those labels. We must accept and come to terms with our emotions: our fears and anxieties about a troubled marriage; our anxieties about our mortality when we receive a physical diagnosis; our fears about a mental health diagnosis, which for me represented a doomsday sentence of taking medication for the rest of my life; or the feelings of inadequacy caused by learning challenges or attentional issues, which make us allergic to special education labels. Personally, I didn't consider the feelings of loneliness and self-loathing that fueled my alcoholism for years.

Labels cause us to face hard conversations about what those labels mean for us as men. Naming something forces us to process the emotions those labels cause us to endure. But for Jacob, and for me, naming it was the first step in taming it.

TIPS FOR GUYS

To master yourself, know and accept your strengths and weaknesses. Ignoring parts of yourself limits your growth.

Accepting one's label is the prescription for the problem. Failure to do so makes people move in the wrong direction, work at cross purposes, and take steps that don't move them closer to goal.

Expect pain on the path to self-acceptance. Embracing hard truths can be tough but opens the way to healing and growth.

TIPS FOR PARENTS

As a parent, expect your son to feel pain when facing tough labels. They carry weight and lasting impact—be ready to support his emotional journey.

Be patient—acceptance takes time and isn't linear. There will be setbacks and then progress; both are part of the journey.

Empathize with your son's journey of self-discovery. Praise his effort and process—not just outcomes—because this work is hard and deserves respect.

LESSON 3

Provision Is Not a Substitute for Presence

Far from solitary

IN MANY remote corners of the world, the journey to manhood is not merely a matter of reaching a certain age; it's a physical and spiritual odyssey marked by time-honored rituals. These rites of passage often involve a young man venturing into the wilderness to hunt for big game, his success or failure determining his status within the tribe. The triumphant return, with a slain beast as evidence of his prowess, signifies his ascension to adulthood and his readiness to take on the responsibilities of a man.

However, this journey is far from solitary. The young hunter is not carelessly "thrown to the wolves" to face challenges alone. He is mentored and guided by seasoned elders from the clan for his entire life up to this moment, men who have walked the same path themselves. These mentors provide invaluable instruction, sharing their knowledge, strategies, and skills. They offer guidance not only on the physical aspects of the hunt but also on the spiritual and emotional challenges that accompany the transition to manhood. The young man is supported, encouraged, and, when necessary, redirected by these wise elders who stand beside him on his transformative journey.

In our society, rite of passage rituals and the notion of male companionship have dissolved for men. Hundreds of years ago, it was common for occupations to be passed within a family lineage for generations. If you were a blacksmith, it meant your father, your grandfather, and your great-grandfather were also blacksmiths. If you grew up on a farm, you came from a family who had been born on the same farm and whose relatives worked that land for generations. If you had a trade, you learned it from your father, who learned it from his father before him.

Because men grew up in the same family business as their fathers, most things they learned about life were bestowed on them experientially by Dad. They worked side by side with their fathers; they developed a sense of work ethic and gained technical knowledge and skills from them as well. Given that our knowledge, technology, and access to the world were so limited hundreds of years ago, information was disseminated from parents to children almost exclusively. What your father knew, you would someday know as well.

But for men, working alongside an elder not only provides

valuable experience and knowledge. It demonstrates favor. It shows that an older man cares for you when he invests his time and shares space with you. It conveys affection, as we like to keep the company of those whom we feel affection toward. Being alongside a younger man also communicates belief in that individual. The implicit notion is that investing your time, as an older male figure, in that younger man is worthwhile, because he, subsequently, is worthy. These messages have tremendous and permanent value for the young man who is receiving them.

These not-so-subtle nonverbals eventually help us form a strong self-concept as young men. They show us that our capacity is high, so much so that older men are willing to invest in us. They teach us the value of discipline and the benefit of investing in ourselves because if older men, especially our dads, will invest in us, then we most certainly should do the same. When young men share time and space with men, they not only learn valuable life skills and gain experience; they learn that they matter, they are worthy, and they should demand the best of themselves. Simply put, when our dads are present and invested fathers, we become better versions of ourselves.

A changing work culture

The world and our access to it are constantly changing and evolving at an ever-increasing pace. Interestingly, this rapid development has impacted the relationships between fathers and sons. In today's fast-paced, "keep up with the Joneses" society, fathers are often preoccupied with work and other responsibilities, leaving them with limited time to engage with their sons. Unlike previous generations, modern fathers rarely work alongside their sons, teach them essential life skills, or take on the primary responsibility of guiding them into adulthood and instilling a code of conduct for navigating the world as young men. As the pace increases, the points of touch within a relationship often disintegrate in accordance.

I see this type of distance especially with the population of affluent suburban males with whom I've worked for nearly the last twenty years. The pressures of high-status, high-stress executive jobs require more time and attention than the typical forty-hour work week. With work email and connectivity to our jobs in our pockets and at our fingertips twenty-four hours a day, gone are the days of nine-to-five employment. The increased distractions among working parents have set the scene for fewer points of touch with their children. Thus, the fathers who send me their sons—to coach them, support them, guide them, mentor them, and pour into them, jobs that were once more typical of dads—are usually working. They're traveling around the world and sitting in high-profile board meetings. More often than I care to admit, they're living in another city Sunday through Thursday, flying home on Friday, then shipping out again that Sunday for another five days of nonstop work. Or maybe Dad lives locally and is around—but he really isn't present. He is inaccessible to his wife and children all day long. He's gone before his kids get on the school bus in the morning and home after his little ones are in bed.

I know how draining that pace can be for a man and his family, not only because I have observed it and its consequences thousands of times, but because I lived it. This occurred over a seven-year span when we first started our business, and it likely contributed to my marriage blowing up before I began to retool my life and make different choices.

The consequences of that workaholism, while intoxicating, are devastating. Fathers and men are so stressed and so overwhelmed by the demands of their jobs that they come home and can't be emotionally available to anyone. Often, these men are angry, irritable, and confrontational at best—downright abusive at worst. As a result, when they are around, moms feel like their absentee husbands are disruptive to the systems and cadence of the household and emotionally unhealthy and potentially harmful for the kids to be around. In general, moms often feel like it's easier to do without Dad. It's easy for Dad to feel Mom's resistance and potentially disdain, too, so it's unsurprising that Dad chooses to work even more. The cycle continues, and the distance between Dad and his children only expands.

An egg

We have a gym adjacent to our office in Westport, Connecticut. The guys and I all work out there; it's a great facility, never crowded, and it provides convenient access for us to get a sweat in during the day to break up our sessions. One morning, in between appointments, I walked next door for a quick run on the treadmill before my next guy. CNBC was on the TV, and since my tech skills are limited, I had no choice but to leave it on to accompany me during my jog.

To my surprise, the familiar face of a client's dad popped up during the finance segment of the morning show. He was being interviewed by a team of reporters after an earnings beat for his Fortune 100 company. He spoke proudly for several minutes, his voice filled with enthusiasm, about the various factors that had contributed to the remarkable growth of his firm's profits. He delved into the specifics of their innovative marketing strategies, the successful launch of new products, and the expansion into untapped markets. He highlighted the dedication and hard work of his team, emphasizing their crucial role in achieving these outstanding results. Frankly, the feat was impressive. He had managed to deliver incredible results in a short period of time.

But the double-digit profit growth wasn't what astounded me. What had me reeling was the fact that an hour before, his son was in my office kitchen, where I had just taught him how to fry an egg. He was twenty-seven years old, and he didn't know how to make himself breakfast. And while his father led his "team" to a multimillion dollar victory, his son was struggling to navigate the most basic of life skills.

I could tell stories like these for days.

A senior in high school worked superhumanly hard and won a spot as a starter in his last year of football. He had an interception that he returned for a touchdown to win the game against his arch rival, but Dad missed it because he was stuck on a flight back from Texas, where he resided from Sunday through Thursday.

An executive who sold his company for $90 million two years ago had worked one hundred hours per week for the last several years to get across the finish line, and when his wife left him the year after he sold his business, all four of his children moved in with her and refused to see or speak to their dad. According to my client, "We barely knew the guy."

Truth is, provision is not a substitute for presence. Dad, your wife and your kids just need you around, no matter how many zeros are at the end of your paycheck or your bank balance, whether it seems like they want you around or not. But that truth comes with an asterisk: They want you around provided you are a good version of yourself. If you are not, they may in fact be better off without you, as you may be thinking to yourself while reading this.

I mentioned how intoxicating the notion of provision can be. As a young man with a fledgling business, I felt the pressures to provide for my family that many men experience. I was chased by the ghosts of growing up with less than, and I was desperate to deliver the kind of life I'd never had and build something my wife and my kids could be proud of. But I made compromises that I never should have, missed things that I deeply regret, and became a version of myself that I'm not proud of.

No matter where you are on that road, or how far off-track you've drifted, it's not too late. The next two stories demonstrate why I know that's true.

As goes the head, so goes the neck

In the early phases of Causeway, I didn't know how to lead people, run an organization, or be a businessman. Intuitively, I had always been very good at "the work," which I define as the amalgamation of my efforts to connect with, draw from, and mold the behaviors of young men. That pursuit is a fairly equal blend of therapy, mentorship, and coaching, which became the pillars of our service offerings at Causeway over the last dozen-plus years. For much of that time, I was a technician—and a damn good one. I took pride in my work and succeeded far more than I failed. Time and again, I witnessed meaningful progress among a resistant population. I even managed to connect with the highly affluent, highly demanding parents who comprised the bulk of our customer base.

Unfortunately, doing the work didn't equip me in any way, shape, or form with the ability to lead others or run an organization with tact, poise, or consistency. In fact, my ability to do the work well (and the ego associated with doing it exceptionally well) actually rendered me less able to lead. As the business grew and expanded, so much of it depended upon my direct service load. So rather than allocate time to teaching, supporting, and coaching others, I left my staff to learn on their own, absent any support.

I became impatient with any questions that arose, and I was reluctant to delegate. There were days in the early years where I would work for ten, eleven, or as many as fourteen direct service hours consecutively, pulling days that went from 8 a.m. to 10 p.m. without engaging with my staff, training them, supporting them, or even responding to them. At the time, I felt that being very good at the work itself justified my ignoring the other requisite elements of running a business.

Now, I know this tunnel vision made me fully unapproachable. In the early days, margins were thin, and I was always stressed about pulling in enough new clients and billing enough hours to keep the lights on. The truth is that young men ages sixteen to thirty are really difficult to provide therapeutic services for. In fact, they are the riskiest clinical population that exists, period, exhibiting the highest rates of suicide, substance use, and violent and/or criminal behavior. As an organization, our collective talent and skill as a team covered for a great many ills, the absence of my leadership in the workplace looming largest of all.

In that phase of my life, my behaviors also revealed glaring issues at home. In short, I was gone—always. My standard hourly work week was in the seventy to seventy-five-hour range for at least the first seven years of the business. My phone was on and I answered it, always. My motto of "24/7/365" functioned as a moniker of pride and diligence. I wore it like a badge.

But on the home front, we had three young kids that G was managing without me. She was working full time, fifty-five or more hours per week, outside the organization in her own high-pressure hefty-deliverables marketing and finance role. She was overwhelmed herself, but instead of us coming together for collective support, my actions pushed her away. In turn, I felt cast aside and unconsidered. I blamed her, often for choices she made without my overt blessing.

The illusions of provision

I didn't see then what is so highly evident now: In the absence of leadership at home and at work, people continued to function and did what they had to; they made decisions to meet their needs and fill in missing information.

At work, this meant guys not asking questions out of fear that they'd be chastised. It meant guys not asking for help when they needed it, which created more frequent mistakes, more cleanup, and more costs in the long run. Rather than clean up more messes that might have been avoided if I'd taken the time to be present, I took on more personally, figuring if I wanted something done right, I had to do it myself.

At home, it meant a wife who was outward leaning from our union, resenting me for my long hours, lack of investment, and minimal attentiveness to her and the family. I was operating under the false impression that by providing for the family, I had full license to do whatever I felt was required. Bend rules? Sure. They didn't apply to me anyway. Yell, scream, swear, and threaten? I did that to everyone. Because how you do anything is how you do everything. Pain in the ass client? Insert expletives and "goodbye." I often had altercations with paying clients, specifically the parents of the young men who came to our center. I was tyrannical and volatile, but all in the name of my calling and my purpose. I justified treating people in my life—specifically those who mattered most—unkindly, without investment, and often without respect. But the business was growing, and the money was flowing in. I was providing for my wife and kids while doing the work I felt God put me here to do.

All was well.

Except it wasn't.

My wife and I didn't just wake up one morning and find ourselves to be strangers in one another's home; it was a slow, steady, almost continental drift until we found our marriage at a crossroads. And for all the sacrifice, all the long hours and laser focus, my business was in a poor position as well. We had rifts within the organization, lack of trust, and questions about my consistency. Because how you do one thing is how you do everything.

Peter Scazzero, author of *The Emotionally Healthy Leader,* talks about leadership as a barometer of influence. For him, everyone possesses leadership in some measure, but the volume, degree, and strength of that influence determine how effective a leader truly is.

For me, retrospectively, I was channeling my influence solely in the domain of direct service work. Based upon those client relationships and their outcomes, clearly I had an influence there. However, I slowly began to recognize that by focusing that influence exclusively on my career limited my ability to spread my time, energy, and efforts to places where they were more important. My marriage suffered. My friendships were nonexistent. I was completely disconnected from my team. I missed my kids and felt like I didn't know them. Things needed to change.

How to start fixing it

It was a brutal pill to swallow; it meant a great many changes needed to happen on my side before I could course correct. One, I needed to make amends to my staff at work. I needed to acknowledge that I had not done right by them in order to initiate the longer process of changing their perceptions of me. They didn't trust me, but only because I didn't give them reason to. They didn't feel safe around me, which was reasonable, given the volatility of my emotional responses.

To fix their perception of me, I had to humble myself—their fearless leader, highly skilled, always working, seemingly infallible. I had to begin by owning my blind spots, my lack of care, my impatience. We needed to reset the culture by building solutions as a unit. In the absence of clarity, people fill in their own information. I needed to own that my guys had the right to ask questions, that it was my responsibility to hear them and answer them well. If you're the guy in charge, people will follow both a good and a bad example; my guys picked up too many bad habits from me. It was my job to initiate the hard reset.

In order to do that, my consistent presence and investment were the foundational ingredients. But I also needed to put my money where my mouth was. We needed to increase the cohesion in the workplace, cultivate joint buy-in, and make people understand they were valuable contributors to a much bigger whole. We started taking steps. We wrote, with the help of the team, our policies and procedures. We crafted a vision statement with the guys' help. I developed a ten-year timeline, outlining the vision of the business over the next decade, practically applied. I established weekly office hours so guys could drop in and talk about, well, anything. I wanted to hear their questions and feedback and pushed them to speak transparently about their impressions. My presence helped the shift in culture.

As challenging as my work was, the real battle was on the home front. G and I were not in a good place. As with the office, the first step was for me to be around, at least to the degree that I could hunker down and do the work. Money and helping my clients did not matter if I wasn't around, available, present, and connected to my wife and my family.

That battle—the quest of winning back my wife's favor—is a separate story to tell, and it will come later, but thankfully there's a happy ending with G and me.

The key takeaway on the home front is that once I acknowledged we were in trouble, not only was I willing to raise my hand and take responsibility for my role, but I was willing to put my time and money where my mouth was.

In case my own cautionary tale doesn't suffice, here's another story of how shifting your responsibilities as a father and beginning to be present with your son can have monumental returns for your relationship.

The Case of Billy

I DIDN'T UNDERSTAND the depths of the issues Billy was facing back then, nor could I have. At a young age, Billy witnessed the erosion of his parents' tumultuous relationship. He was traumatized by the conflict that ensued as he observed powerful and volatile episodes of reciprocal abuse between his parents. He and his two siblings had very close relationships, mostly as a result of the conflict that they witnessed for their formative years and the necessity they found in sticking together in the midst of so much chaos.

From Jump Street, I never liked Billy's dad. His father presented as incredibly intact: intelligent, highly successful, and charming. Personally, I saw through it. Dad's well-dressed attire gave him shades of wisdom and a countenance I couldn't compete with. His elegant salt and pepper hair and kind eyes were topped off with a delightful British accent that made it hard to imagine him as flawed or disengaged. He was the epicenter of the room when he walked in. His grandiosity conveyed the self-love that his appearance itself carried.

Dad was a big shot who was the true definition of a self-made guy; he grew up on the streets of London selling drugs and fistfighting his way around the city for survival. Despite the polish in his voice and the gravitas that being both handsome and British conveyed, he was a street guy—a bad dude and tough as nails at his core.

Billy's dad's saving grace was that he was one hell of an athlete. The only reason he found his way out of the streets of Westminster was because he could kick the hell out of a soccer ball. He was whip smart and didn't have to work very hard in high school, and he was able to win a scholarship to play soccer at a Big East school. There, he was the definition of the big man on campus.

Billy's dad jumped right into working like crazy after graduation, plowing ahead from the ground up at a real estate development firm. This man possessed what some who chase money don't: a deep-rooted desire for the trappings of wealth and a willingness to sacrifice his life at home with his wife and kids to achieve it. As a result, more than twenty years later, he boasted what most people aspire to obtain: a C-suite job with one of the largest real estate developers in New York City. He had enough cash to stroke a check and pay in full for his kids to go to college. He had a seat on the board of trustees where two of his kids attended school, which, by the way, most likely resulted in his son's acceptance to the very same university. Dad was a scholarship athlete himself. He had a house in the Hamptons. An apartment in the city. And enough cash that it was often referenced aloud in our sessions together. Dad had a huge job and a huge ego to match. Again, his self-importance and ego were repellent for me. They were, however, very effective in shielding outsiders from how he showed up to his family behind closed doors.

But Billy's mom was the clue that tipped me to his pain. She, unfortunately, was an unmitigated disaster. She had an adorable face and bright blue sparkling eyes that offset her platinum blond high ponytail. But she took to alcohol in mass quantity when the issues with her husband began.

The divorce

When his parents' marriage went to pieces, Billy started to decompensate. He found out his father was having an affair with his secretary; frequent business trips to Savannah to work on a project for the firm were actually Dad canoodling with his mistress in his hotel room. They covered their tracks for years, but eventually, as most people do, Mom found out what was going on.

I give her a lot of credit for leaving. She held him accountable. There had been whispers of previous extramarital affairs that she let go by because she didn't have proof, but as soon as she caught him red-handed, she put him out on the street, despite the fact that it was his house, his money, his resources and connections, and, from most people's perspective, his family. Mom had her own mental health issues, and this situation served as the tipping point, causing her to descend into a downward spiral. She, frankly, couldn't accept that Billy's dad had moved on, marrying the very woman with whom he'd had an affair for the back half of their marriage. For her, that wound never healed.

The battle for custody of the kids and control of the assets was more than tumultuous, even after the divorce was almost finalized. The family had relocated from the Midwest because of Dad's C-suite job. They'd had a wonderful circle of friends in Indianapolis, and Billy loved it there. At that point, he was a well-adjusted baseball player getting great grades and doing well in nearly every aspect of his life. He had a beautiful girlfriend, and they hung out in age-appropriate, developmentally positive ways. His substance use wasn't even on the horizon at that time.

Poor at best

As a result of the move and the discord at home, Billy's relationships with both of his parents were poor at best. His mom often became frustrated with the conditions of the family system. Dad was not around. As such, she was largely responsible for spotlighting Billy's issues and frequently spoke out to me when she had concerns. Ultimately, Mom worked persistently and without yield to retrain Billy's previous impression that as long as he showed up to work, school, or practice and did an average job, his conduct everywhere else could be excused and rationalized. After all, his dad just made excuses for him. Mom was unwilling to accept that, in spite of her ex-partner who sat back and did so tacitly. She, thankfully, did not.

Clearly, Billy struggled in many ways because of the absence of his father. He missed out on a number of essential lessons that most men learn by observing their dads: how to treat a woman; how to work hard and be patient in pursuit of your goal; how to be consistent with your word; what to do when hard things come your way; how to trust others. How do you know that you matter? Billy never had his father around to reinforce those learning lessons.

Instead, Billy's father afforded his son opportunities that most other kids don't enjoy. A live-in nanny cooked all meals and cleaned for the family so the kids wouldn't have to worry about picking up after themselves. A car service was available to them at their beck and call. When they got older, they had an apartment in Midtown, which they could use to attend amazing events in New York City and then have a safe place to spend the night without the inconvenience of traveling back to Westport. Billy's father exchanged one set of tradeoffs for another, believing the conveniences he afforded his family were more important than his physical presence. In truth, those conveniences enabled his son, robbed him of the opportunity to learn necessary and valuable life skills, and did not compensate for his dad's absence.

Besides Dad not being physically present, the main issue in the system was the incongruence in the perspectives of Billy's mother and father. Mom needed to play bad cop often, holding Billy accountable, conveying her skepticism about the nature of his choices and communicating the essential course corrections in his conduct. Dad, however, had some of his own demons, lots of shame and guilt, and his own substance use history. Because of that, it was essential for Dad, in his own eyes, to maintain a friendship with his son first and foremost and to validate his son's difficulties. I appreciated what he was trying to do; however, at every turn and with every decision, he was undercutting his ex-wife, creating separation between the two of them and further fueling his son's oppositionality. Not a recipe for success.

Stemming from the mixed messages he received and the communication issues between his parents, Billy treated his family with incredible disrespect—his mother, father, and sister alike. He habitually blew up at them, called them heinous names, made threats, and challenged his parents' authority when they tried to intervene. Billy didn't abide by the rules of the household and told his parents where to get off whenever they tried to impose boundaries of any kind.

Our work

As a result of the lack of strong relationships in his life, but specifically with Billy's father and mother, Billy and I focused our time on building his interpersonal and relational skills. On a weekly basis during our calls, we discussed his attempts at romantic relationships, which really meant we examined his futile attempts to pick up girls with empty one-liners that fell flat, and we examined his ego as a result of sustaining yet another blow. But I pressed him to work to instill an understanding of his inner constitution. Why did he need to rely on alcohol in order to feel loose and confident? What motivated him to trivialize his interactions with women? What forced him to approach girls in ways they didn't respond to? Questions such as these within mentorship, rendered in smaller, twenty- to thirty-minute conversations on a more frequent basis over the arc of the week, created a through line to more meaningful discussion over time. My approach helped me move slowly ahead as I earned his trust, paying homage to his lack of relationship with other adults in his life.

As we pressed on, we reviewed each interaction with both young men and young women from the past weekend. We identified and discussed alternative ways in which Billy could have steered the conversation, as well as his underlying motivation to handle it in the fashion he chose. Over time, Billy began to build a deeper willingness to pause and consider the implications of his choices before acting. These were conversations Billy had most certainly never had with his dad.

Billy and I also spent time on tangible and discrete Therapeutic Mentorship interventions that helped him organize his life, reduce chaos in his mind, and solidify his routine. We built a weekly calendar and schedule for him to assist in managing his free time, thinking and planning ahead, and making appointments, as his executive functioning was poor and he also had an ADHD diagnosis. We came up with a workout routine and schedule, operating under the belief that wellness work would help manage both his mood and increase his energy. We also saw fitness as a means for him to decrease stress, thus limiting conflict with his parents and helping him make less impulsive choices when feeling the urge to be aggressive. Whereas most men learn how to manage their time from watching their parents, this was a nice opportunity to introduce Billy to novel information. It was also clear that what I taught him could effectively assist him in managing his time and his responsibilities.

It was evident through my insider's perspective on the family system that Dad's emotional and physical absence took a toll on everyone, Billy most of all. Dad had recently stopped drinking, upon receiving an ultimatum from his second wife, who, like his ex-wife before her, had enabled years of substance use and angry outbursts at home. Dad clearly had a high-stress job, and managing the real estate endeavors of multibillionaires is no easy role. Billy's dad didn't wear it well.

By the time I came on board to help his kid, Dad was beginning to be more transparent about how his challenges had plagued his family. In spite of his bravado, I had earned Dad's trust, and because of that, he was willing to be open about the work he'd put in during his own therapeutic process. He also conceded that the work needed to continue because of the scope of the damage he had caused his family. He shared his newfound desire for change in an effort to bring his family closer together. Compared with his lack of past effort, he was certainly doing better, and he was trying.

As Billy's dad recalibrated their relationship and worked on being present, he had the unique opportunity to override Billy's poor behaviors and model new ones.

Based upon my feedback over the arc of our work, Billy's dad saw the influence he had over his son and the necessity of taking hard-line positions when it mattered, even when Billy was upset. This change in posture forced him to come alongside his ex-wife and support her position, even if they don't typically get along. Dad also understood the value of his time, not just his money. Now, he and his son spend more time together. They grab dinner together a couple times per month and have gone to a couple of New York sporting events together. Unsurprisingly, they report getting along much better. I don't see that as a coincidence.

Since Dad has been around more, things seem to be getting better between him and Billy's mom, too. He's more mindful now of not undermining his former partner. Rather than addressing their grievances with Billy directly, they come together and engage in productive discussion prior to bringing their issues to Billy. Their ability to join and communicate well and without blame has led to massive strides in the consistency of their parenting. Sure, their relationship has its wounds, but those are healing too. Recently, they've even been aligned clearly and concisely on the list of items Billy must satisfy prior to moving out of Mom's home, with Dad's financial support.

Absence vs. presence

Billy and his family came into my care suffering from an intense bout of Affluenza. This top-down, systemic culture within their household instilled in this young man a belief system that elevated his own self-importance, stripped him of personal accountability and autonomy, and created a framework where he was perpetually enabled by his parents. Prior to our work together, Billy learned he could do the bare minimum required of him and continue to be rewarded by the world around him because his parents insisted upon doing the heavy lifting in his life. These days, Billy has a relationship with both his parents. He's not as angry as he used to be. He has accomplished things, like obtaining and working a job, saving money, and identifying a place that he can afford on a budget. As his parents have taken more active roles in his life, we've all seen how much their joint presence can yield for him as a young man.

Exposure

In the process of exposure, boys receive the opportunity to be fathered by men, not only their biological fathers but other older men in their lives, like coaches, teachers, and community or religious leaders. These men will provide feedback that will either begin to solidify maladaptive behaviors or redirect toward more favorable alternatives. When boys receive affirmation from the group for maladaptive behaviors, however, it becomes solidified in their memory, and those behaviors will continue on a loop until they are disrupted and redirected.

Here, it is essential for the father (or parent) to wield his influence wisely and work to instill principles, values, and morals that can override poor behavior while providing a map of which decisions make the most sense and why. Within an ideal framework, a boy will always be most affected by the feedback and direction of his own father. A present and committed father possesses the greatest opportunity for fostering behavioral change because of the frequency of interactions, proximity within relationships, and biological sameness.

Men often get it wrong in terms of evaluating the necessity of their being around. At times, when it seems Mom can handle everything seamlessly and in an organized and productive way, dads diminish their personal importance to the family unit. Because their career is highly affirming, labeled as being important or financially gratifying, a magnetic pull redirects them toward the work domain and away from the drudgery and frustration of the household. Particularly when he is not present as much as Mom, Dad's contributions at home, particularly in matters of conflict, can seem disruptive. Young men need the relationship that only their fathers can provide, and in the absence of a father's influence, they cannot be ushered into manhood in ways that allow them to become their best selves.

However, provision is not a substitute for presence. Your kids will do what you *do* far before they will do what you *say*. Young men will learn how to *be* from whatever surrounds them. Proximity teaches them how to respond, how to act when frustrated, what manners look like, and what their values are—all this comes from small-scale exposures in a young man's environment. Your son will either learn directly from you or from the world at large.

A good version of you as a parent will give you the opportunity to filter that message. A version that is not present cannot.

TIPS FOR GUYS

Time matters most. Prioritize spending it with your loved ones, and show your family they're your top priority.

Manhood is shaped through guidance and rituals shared with other men. Mentorship and connection are essential to identity and growth.

Focus on intention, not just outcome. Even if a dad's presence feels lacking, his intentions often come from a good place while he navigates his own challenges.

TIPS FOR PARENTS

Work expectations have changed, especially with remote work. Guard against being overly available to your job so you can stay present for your partner and kids.

Set clear work boundaries. Communicate which nights are family time, and protect those moments as sacred.

It's never too late to repair father-son relationships. With accountability, forgiveness, and consistent effort, even deep wounds can heal.

LESSON 4

Find Your Inner Wild

Born to be Wild

WHEN my wife's best friend had a baby, we went to see their beautiful new family at their new home. The baby girl was a tiny little peanut, only two weeks old.

As beautiful as that newborn bundle of joy was, though, the most noteworthy takeaway that sunny winter afternoon was the behavior of the older brother. His folks told us they were having a rough time with him.

I wasn't sure that I believed the degree of trouble she was describing, so I headed up the stairs to do my own reconnaissance.

I arrived at the top of the staircase and was greeted by a cohort of four boys, posted up behind a locked baby gate: Two of them were mine, one the older brother of the newborn baby, and the other the nephew of my wife's other best girlfriend. Four boys ages twelve, ten, eight, and two. All four grilling me as I approached. The scene was very *Lord of the Flies,* which only amplified my curiosity.

The two-year-old brother, now shirtless, stepped immediately to the forefront of the group to confront the perceived threat.

"Hey bud," I said, conveying a tone of positivity and curiosity. "Can I come up and hang with you boys?"

As fast as the last syllable was uttered out of my mouth, it was Dikembe-Mutomboed right back at me with a firm "No!" complete with a textbook Dikembe finger wag. The little guy did not appreciate my breaking up of his boys' club. This was met with uniform laughter from his three elder mates. But the bigger surprise was that the little guy then wound up and tried to slap me, followed by yet another firmly exclaimed "No!"

I put my hand on the little guy's shoulder and said, "Buddy, we can't hit people," but the damage was done. The rest of his cronies were yukking it up behind him. His Wildness had been celebrated and affirmed by the other members of his crew.

As the day passed, his mother elaborated on her concerns. Obviously, I didn't snitch on the little guy for taking a swing at me, because as they say in *Goodfellas,* the worst thing you can be in life is a snitch, but I did probe to find out if such behaviors were part of a larger pattern.

"He's just really hard right now," his mom said. "He throws things all over the house, makes messes, roughhouses constantly, climbs all over everything, and every single word out of his mouth is no. What do we do?"

"I'm actually not sure it's such a bad thing," I responded.

The pull

There's something that pulls at the inner being of every male regardless of their age and phase of life.

That pull is their desire to be Wild. To return to our roots as men. To experience freedom, unbridled and without parameters. To be one with nature and seek to connect with our primal elements. To be devoid of rules, restrictions, and fear. To live in community and in deep interconnectedness with one another and with the world around us.

What is it about the Wild that pulls at the soul of a boy? Or a young man? And what happens to that notion of the Wild across the lifespan? The Wild provides the forum for a man to test himself, to see what he's made of, and to evaluate himself against the feet of his predecessors and peers. In nature, there are no limits, no written rules that govern who we are as men and how we should operate.

When you build that bike jump as a boy that rockets you into the clouds, there's no blueprint for how tall you can make it, no limitations on how high you can soar. When you're firing down a hill on an alpine ski slope, no guidelines other than gravity dictate how fast you can rip it down to base camp. Even when you're doing pushups in gym class, no one decides when to stop except you.

Yes, the Wild is encapsulated by all things nature, but it's more than just that. The Wild can be any venue in which we stare into a blank canvas and face the limitations of the self.

It is there that we can measure our worth, evaluate how we stack up against those of previous generations and previous experiences, and seek to gain the favor of our elders. In that Wild, the outcome is unknown; we are both completely exposed and forced to be fully trusting of our inner Wild.

Sucking out our Wild ...

And yet, the world sucks the Wild out of us as men. As we have children, buy minivans, and engage in the trappings of all things domestic, the Wild doesn't manifest in the day-to-day. It's hard to feel your inner Wild when you're baking chocolate chip cookies, shuttling girls back and forth to ballet classes, or sitting in a cubicle doing redundant and mundane work that makes you feel like your soul is being extracted from your being.

Even worse, there are those men (you know the type) who present as the disgruntled husband. "Yeah, well ... it would be nice if I could do x, y, or z, but the ole ball and chain will lose her mind." Or further emasculating comments like, "I used to spend money on that, but my wife's got my 'you know whats' in a vice" or some other trope that presents both a lack of unity as well as an innate resentment of the institution of marriage.

Nothing feels less Wild than a subpar marriage, and I feel bad for people who exist within one. I say that because I used to exist within a marriage filled with old resentments, disrespectful commentary, restrictions, and lack of freedom. It was devoid of life-giving encouragement. If you want to unlock your inner Wild, start with your relationship. Eliminate the conventional rules that govern partnership more broadly. Infuse the dynamic with spontaneity. Play. Sit still. Dream.

The more we eliminate our own personal limitations from the framework of a monotonous relationship, the more we can begin to re-engage with our inner Wild.

So what are we aiming for?

Being Wild requires work that unlocks the soul of a man. It deeply saddens me to see a man who so clearly has a calling that God has put on his life that he has chosen not to pursue. Sometimes that redirection away from the work of the soul happens for noble reasons: A wife is pregnant or a family member is sick, and a man has to pick up more stable work for better pay with more consistent hours and insurance benefits.

While those are noble reasons to shift one's work focus, I've done career work with men and young men for long enough that I can see almost immediately when a man is sitting in a chair in the professional realm that he should not be inhabiting. What I can say, from both observation and experience, is that living outside of his calling deeply limits a man's potential in being who God intended him to become. Additionally, it limits the energy, power, leadership, and influence he carries, further diminishing his potential to be a life source for others. This is where we see elder men, and specifically fathers, demonstrating diminished capacity in their respective ability to speak life-affirming words to the younger generation.

Maybe the biggest issue of all is confusion about how to hold being Wild alongside being good. Society, culture, music, conventional norms—all of these avenues have muddled and commingled what the meaning of a man is, let alone a good man. Is a good man one who works ninety hours per week to provide a life of affluence for his family? Is a good man a stay-at-home dad who handles all the household domestic responsibilities but doesn't bring home a paycheck? Is a good man single, no wife and children of his own, but functioning as a father figure to his nieces and nephews? Is a good man a grandfather who pays for his grandchildren to go to college but lives in Boca and only sees them twice a year?

More confounding is the nebulous "bad boy" notion conjured up by the construct of being Wild. Is Wild the snowboarder who gets airlifted and dropped by helicopter into five feet of fresh powder on a remote mountaintop? Is it the rapper who curses and threatens to shoot people in every other line of his music and tells stories of his sexual conquests after his shows? Is it the mountain climber who solos without the aid of ropes? Is it the Boy Scout who has earned every survival badge under the sun and could survive more effectively in the wilderness than any of his peers, who label him a "nerd" nonetheless? It's hard to identify a path toward maintaining our inner Wild when we don't even know what bullseye we're aiming for.

Is there any Wild within them at all?

Yet another concern when it comes to this generation of young men is that there will be no Wild within them at all. Rather than seeing men with their eyes looking up, both to the heavens, where the God of the universe calls home, and the horizon, where all possibilities arise, I observe a generation of young men with their heads down, so much so that the curvature of the human spine has been decreasing in its degree since cell phones became accessible to the mass market. According to Dr. Todd Lanman, a spinal neurosurgeon at Cedars-Sinai Medical Center in Los Angeles, "In an X-ray the neck typically curves backward, and what we're seeing is that the curve is being reversed as people look down at their phones for hours each day."

Boys are failing out of college in record numbers. Boys are isolated to an extent never seen in human history. Boys are so plagued by anxiety and fear that they don't even want to drive, let alone drive too fast. Boys can't muster up the courage to ask a girl for her number or take a girl on a date out of fear that their buddy will give them grief because no one goes on dates anymore. We live in a "play it safe" world. We live in a "don't drive at all, just have your mother drop you off instead" world. We live in a world where we won't even make friends because we're frightened to be rejected. All this represents the opposite of Wild. It sucks. And it's sad.

So how do we find our Wild? And if we are lucky enough to do so, how do we sustain it? How do we protect it from the world robbing us of this lifeforce? I have some examples of what I believe is right in cultivating Wild in young men. But first, here's a story about how I lost my Wild and found it again to demonstrate how easily this essential life force comes and goes if we don't meticulously tend to it.

Dialing for dollars

When I met my wife and fell in love with her immediately, I was instinctually pulled by the conventional notion of provision. Despite knowing I wanted to help others and fully believing I was called by this work, Gina was my primary point of emphasis. I had big plans for us, plans that involved me making a ton of money as a cornerstone ingredient. These plans, however, represented my migrating farther away from a dream of doing altruistic work humbly rendered in service to others. This was and remains my calling. It is no coincidence that as soon as I started drifting away from it, I could feel that something wasn't quite right.

But at that point, I didn't care. Pursuing my calling (down a road that began with grossly inadequate earning potential for me) was a dream already abandoned anyhow, based upon pivoting away from nonprofit work and into an entry-level job in sales. For me, big corporate felt like moving into the horribly bland but sufficiently lucrative sales work I was already doing, but with a greater upside—more money and fast-tracking what already felt like a fast track. It was the obvious next step at the time.

Unfortunately, this next step—into the big leagues of corporate sales—only drew me farther from who I was at my core, and who I wanted to be. I had to coexist with people I didn't like, talk about superficial nonsense I wasn't interested in, and again, do work that I didn't care about at all. I was "dialing for dollars," boiler-room style.

I was at my desk at 7 a.m. Didn't put the phone down except for bathroom breaks and a thirty-minute lunch. Three hundred-plus calls per day, every day. Dialing line managers, VPs, HR reps, and C-suite executives to gather information on their internal operations, pitch temporary staffing services to move through busy seasons, and whenever possible, sell permanent hires at the right place at the right time.

The work was thankless, but I attacked it with everything I had, every day. I planned for the next day from 5 p.m. to 6:30

p.m. I studied until 7 p.m. since I was a recruiter working in the financial services industry and didn't know anything at all about financial services. On top of that, this was 2008—right smack in the middle of the worst financial crisis in this country since the Great Depression. And I was trying to sell people temporary employees in financial services. Not optimal market conditions, to say the least.

I was giving it all I had, but I was absolutely miserable. Think "pit in your stomach every Sunday because you have to wake up the next morning and do a week's worth of soul-crushing work and you have no idea how you're going to make it through" kind of miserable. At this point, it was early 2009, and G and I had only been married for three months. Our wedding had been huge (310 guests), with a big sticker price to match. I felt awful about the fact that only a couple of months later, after we had received such overwhelming support (mostly from her folks, but from others too), G and I found ourselves in a situation of budding financial hardship if I left the company. And with a mortgage, by the way.

Pack your stuff and go

Gina knew how unhappy I was at work, but she also knew how prideful and stubborn a man I could be. She had already communicated her desire to see me leave my job in corporate recruiting, even though I didn't have a backup plan. For her, it was far more important that I show up positive, calm, and consistent rather than anxious and snippy due to my work issues, even if the salary mattered for us at the time. She would have rather seen a man who was poor and Wild than one who was boring, agitated, easily frustrated, and a shell of himself.

"I'm sorry, G, but I can't do this anymore," I said, violently wiping tears from my eyes to maintain my composure. I couldn't allow myself to lose it in our corner booth of the Panera Bread where we met for lunch across the street from her office. "I can't work with people who are like this, doing work I can't stand. I'm miserable every day. But I can't bring myself to walk away." At that time, I valued honoring my commitments and the notion of provision more than I did my own freedom, peace, and spirit.

"Leave, V. Pack your stuff and go. You've been unhappy for months, and I don't want to be married to someone who's miserable. Quit. And leave." Her words, as I write them, feel almost prophetic. *I don't want to be married to someone who's miserable.* Back then, my love for her was held tight, front and center. So I listened to her. She knew me too well to advise me to stay knowing the depths of my dissatisfaction.

So I put my belongings in a box that afternoon and left. I didn't even say goodbye to people I worked with. I realized in an instant that I could never be in a workplace with people I didn't trust or care for. Come to think of it, it's probably why I value those things so much in the workplace now, and why we put so much into creating a culture and space where employees can grow, thrive, and feel supported.

Finding my Wild again

The reason I lost my Wild in the first place is because in chasing conventional notions of provision (in isolation not necessarily a bad thing), I migrated away from my calling and toward making money for making money's sake. This is a common snare that entangles men as the Wild is sapped from their being. That life and lifestyle sucked the juice out of me for a few reasons.

First, that work was the opposite of being brave. One can never be Wild when he is afraid. Personally, fear and anxiety plagued my countenance and my spirit in this setting. On a regular basis, I saw things I knew were wrong and suppressed my desire to communicate about them for fear of making waves. Not speaking up about something that is wrong and being a passive bystander to a process where someone is being harmed or what is right is being ignored represents the opposite of Wild and cannot occur, irrespective of context or upside. Now, part of my Wild in my work is that I always get the opportunity to do the right thing: I get to oppose people who take the wrong position, and I have the opportunity to advocate for those who cannot advocate for themselves. Doing what is right, surprisingly, is core to maintaining our Wild. Selling out, in whatever form, represents the opposite.

Second, there was no freedom for creative expression and for connecting with my soul by doing things differently. Here, the work was far too bridled with far too many parameters. The approach was painstakingly methodical, slow and poky in the pace of both the sell cycle and the personal gains someone could make. It was highly regimented and skills driven. The hours were the same every day, the approach and structure were the same every day, and meetings were held with the same tonality, the same metrics examined. Hearing the same people saying the same things eroded my fortitude. Part of being Wild and being able to connect with one's calling is the freedom to express oneself. One of the most beautiful things about Causeway is how creative and individualized the work is with every client we see. No client is the same, so no approach is the same, and even among the team, no two people approach the same circumstance in an identical fashion. In sum, freedom is a requisite for maintaining one's Wild, and no structure that embodies sameness, consistency, monotony, and boredom can provide an avenue to maintain the Wild inside of a man. If a man finds himself in that workplace culture, he needs to look elsewhere to nourish his soul.

Finally, being Wild involves living in community and in deep interconnectedness with one another and with the world around us. At my corporate recruiting job, I did work that didn't matter to me in the company of people I didn't respect. I became almost unrecognizable, shedding all individuality, personality, and uniqueness that made me, well, me. Instead, I dressed like the guys to my left and right, spoke like them, even bent my principles and morals to compete with them, seeking to achieve a goal that, other than compiling money, didn't resonate with me. The work didn't challenge me; it wasn't difficult, but it felt unfulfilling. With every passing day, the job pulled me farther from who I was and certainly farther from being the man G fell in love with.

She was drawn to my Wild, my spontaneity, my energy, my willingness to take risks, my toughness, and my honesty. Instead, she found herself in the presence of a guy who became anxious, fearful to speak his mind, bland and muted with respect to creative expression, and who started posturing like a know-it-all who actually knows very little. In essence, the Wild was beaten out of me, slowly and steadily, as I abandoned my proclivity for rugged individualism and wandered instead down a path of conformity and passivity.

Fortunately, not only did I jump ship in time to set both my career and my life on the right trajectory, but I've been blessed with the opportunity to share space with young men from whom we can all learn something about how to never abandon their Wild, irrespective of circumstance. One such story is the case of Jimmy, who found his Wild in the most unlikely of places, on the most unlikely of personal journeys.

The Case of Jimmy

When I first met Jimmy, I was fairly certain he was high. Back then, he usually was. He came to see me for the first time at fifteen years old, wearing an oversized sweatshirt, the bill of his hat tipped over his eyes, and his pants hanging off his backside. He walked like a punk, talked like a punk, dressed like a punk, and swore like a punk. This was a kid who I immediately knew I would relate to and get on with swimmingly.

It was pretty obvious from talking to Jimmy for a snap that he was whip smart. He didn't do well in school; in fact, when I met him, he was failing every single one of his classes. That, however, had absolutely nothing to do with him lacking aptitude. Jimmy just never did anything, literally anything. He never did his work, never handed in his homework, and never went to class, instead choosing to slide his way out behind the courtyard and sell weed while he smoked pot with his buddy Joe and many of the other upperclassmen (by the way, Joe would find his own way to me later that year).

Jimmy started to decompensate when his parents' marriage went to pieces. There was volatility, aggressive communication, verbal abuse, confusion, lies, cheating, and uncertainty that created chaos in the system for all of the kids, especially Jimmy. He was not only his father's golden boy, to put it mildly, but also the person everyone relied upon to keep the peace. When he failed to do so, Jimmy felt the pressure from everybody and started to fall apart. As a result, he turned to drugs to numb out and disconnect.

I always conceptualized Jimmy's situation as a "substance-primary" presentation. Sure, there was trauma underlying, but really it was the substance use that put Jimmy over the edge. He was using pills pretty much every day by the time we met. He also relied on alcohol at night and smoked weed, too, on more than a regular basis.

Hustle invoked Jimmy's Wild

But that didn't get in the way of his entrepreneurial endeavors. Back then, Jimmy was pushing anything that he could get his hands on to make money. At the time, it was high-end, limited-edition sneakers; then it became designer clothing, which he picked up by waiting in long lines in the Village and then flipped for huge margins on the secondary market. Next, Jimmy moved into crypto, all within about two to three years as he became a fixture in my life and on my caseload.

Being an entrepreneur was the only productive means through which Jimmy experimented with his Wild. He got into verbal altercations with his parents, trying to assert his dominance in a situation at home that he simply could not control. He got into fistfights with people at school, trying to find ways to purge himself of his overly aggressive inclinations. He used substances to excess, attempting to do anything he could to numb his pain. But in starting and running multiple businesses, Jimmy managed new and unforeseen circumstances by himself. He used his creativity as he encountered new situations. He faced adversity and overcame it. He found a venue to flex his intellect in ways that were interest-aligned and values-centered.

When he was young and going off the deep end, it was my job to send him off to drug treatment. But this guy was always tough and immensely resilient, and he was able to put his courage on full display when he returned. He dropped back into his old life, fully immersing himself into the same peer group where his substance use and acting out had begun, but he abstained from using drugs for years. He bought in, went to meetings, said no, affirmed his no when needed, and rolled with the same crowd while holding up his end of the deal. It was remarkable to see the leadership and internal strength that he exhibited at just fifteen years old.

In an ironic twist of fate, Jimmy found his Wild in sobriety, in some respects the most unlikely of places. Before he got sober, Jimmy was a force in the social scene at school, using his magnetism to win the favor of guys who respected him and girls who crushed on him, as the resident bad boy in town. But when he came home, the task in front of him was both novel and more difficult. Jimmy wanted to maintain those same drug-addicted relationships, absent the drugs. Unlike most people who get and remain sober, who, according to AA, have to replace people, places, and things, Jimmy was Wild enough to rewrite the book on what sobriety meant to him. And like he did everything before and everything since, Jimmy did sobriety—but he did it his way. He kept the same friends. He went to the same parties. He maintained his previous interests. He cultivated the respect of peers and the favor of female admirers, but this time, Jimmy did it stone-cold sober. To this day, given his age and the circumstances he faced, there was no badder dude than Jimmy, and no one more Wild at his core.

Lizards?

By 2018, Jimmy had made incredible progress, and he'd also made some decisions about who he wanted to be. As a result, with more than two years of sobriety under his belt, I discharged Jimmy. At that point, he was working, had moved out on his own, had many friends, and had done the work we set out to do. He wasn't quite ready for college, but that was okay. Our work was done, and my door, Jimmy knew, was always open. He was one of those guys I sincerely hoped would take me up on that offer.

Jimmy resurfaced again in late 2020 and came back to me seeking help, feeling depressed from the isolation of COVID, like so many other young men. We've continued to see each other once every six weeks or so, but it's light work now, with a very different tonality and focus.

These days, he's a project manager for a real estate development firm. He's been working there for four years successfully. He's completely turned his life around. He manages his health and wellness. He doesn't drink or smoke pot, and he also has successful relationships. He has friendships. He cares for himself. He goes to the gym. He has both interests and community through his work and the hobbies that sustain him.

But over time, Jimmy felt himself losing pieces of what made him uniquely him. If we're not careful as men to prioritize and nourish the parts of ourselves that function as our Wild, this natural regression happens slowly and steadily over time. Many times, we don't notice until we simply don't recognize ourselves. Jimmy started to get bored at work. He began to feel less motivated to get up for work in the morning, to go to the gym at night, and to get after, well, life with the same fervor he'd always had. The daily grind was getting to him.

Jimmy no longer felt inspired by his work. Many of his buddies went away to college, and the deeply interconnected circle of friends that was once a central force in his life no longer had the same appeal. He started spending more time alone binge-watching Netflix. He wasn't eating as much and lost some weight.

In order for Jimmy to get motivated again, he needed to figure out how to hold on to what had always made him so unique: a deep ability to become passionate about things and pour himself into something to a degree most others simply can't and won't. In sum, Jimmy needed to reconnect with his inner Wild.

Now, Jimmy is smart enough, resourceful enough, and persuasive enough to be good at quite literally anything he decides to do. But not everything would nourish his soul, build out his spirit, and set him on fire. I knew he would be highly skilled at anything he poured himself into, and he would derive tremendous satisfaction from it. Since the day I met him, Jimmy has been an enthusiast for anything he loves.

So these days, his passion isn't sneakers or designer clothes or cryptocurrency. These days, Jimmy found his inner Wild ... *raising lizards!*

"I started a business breeding exotic lizards!" he exclaimed proudly. "I absolutely love it, but I need your help with a business plan and with staying organized."

I wasn't sold ... until I heard him talk about lizards. About their mating habits. About the coloring of their scales. About the temperature of the tanks in order to maximize the likelihood that the clutch of eggs would produce the maximum amount of viable offspring. About how to make enclosures out of PVC and about factories in China he had already contacted about sourcing it.

Jimmy knew everything about lizards. Me? I knew almost nothing. But anyone who cares so much about something that he's willing to independently pursue it in such a devoted, comprehensive, and painstaking manner should be doing that thing as their main thing.

Even more telling than Jimmy's words, however, were his nonverbals. Talking about lizards and PVC and tank temperature and mating habits and the colors of the scales of jeweled geckos lit up his smile like a July sunrise. He gushed with enthusiasm, his hands flailing as he magnificently animated his delivery, his voice beaming with inflection. It wasn't just what Jimmy said, it was the way he said it that sold me. Despite watching Jimmy's interests change over the years, it was obvious when he came back around what our collective end goal should be.

Jimmy, one of the wildest guys I've ever been around, found his inner Wild, right smack in the middle of being forty-five months sober, doing something he never imagined could pull at his heart.

Toddlers, lizards, and guys like me ...

When I reflect back upon our weekend visit with G's friend and her two-year-old son, it makes much more sense with this information in context. Could the boy's behavior be characterized as his acting out? Of course. Yet I think that would discount an innate desire that exists within all boys to win the favor of and learn from older men.

Arriving at the top of the landing to find a two-year-old performing for a group of three boys behind him was as clear an indicator as I can imagine of a boy's need to seek the affirmation of his elders. As I mentioned earlier, in the boyhood phase of development, boys seek the primary affirmation of their fathers to learn, to gain approval, to test themselves and see where they land, and to evaluate their own self-worth. That toddler's swing and a miss was more than just a misdirected punch: It was a grand gesture of seeking acceptance. He wanted to see whether this group of older men would embrace him.

So personally, I'm cool with a two-year-old who rips all the diapers out of the holder and throws them around the living room. I'm cool with that same two-year-old taking a swing at me and telling me through his actions, "Get the hell out of here, pal. I'm chillin' with a bunch of older bros, and they're cool. Stop throwin' shade." I'm cool with that two-year-old riding his three wheeler around the house, crashing into everything at every turn. And even though his parents are completely shot, spread thin, and can't appreciate his Wild in the same way that I can from a distance, I want to remind his mom that it's actually better than the alternative.

He's young.

He's filled with life.

He's curious.

He's learning, and receiving more learning through feedback and guidance when he makes mistakes.

He has fire in his eyes.

Which is why I'm cool with Jimmy's story, big mess to clean up and all. And the up and down road I walked alongside him. Because even though he was angry, acting out, and often misdirected, he was damn sure passionate about nearly everything. And even as he became more mature and followed a more traditional path as he got life together, Jimmy never stopped searching for his Wild. Jimmy was also brave enough to accept that he found it in an unlikely place, but he was never ashamed to share what he found with others.

I'm not upset, these days at least, that I lost my Wild in order to find it again. Once I recognized that staying at that job was the greatest threat to being the man I wanted to become, the choice to jump ship became easy. What I regarded for a while as quitting and walking away actually required far more courage and bravery than staying the course. And jumping into the unknown is a fantastic way to give your life that lacks Wild the boost of adrenaline it desperately needs.

So if you want a crash course in finding your Wild, take a leap of faith and do something brave, like walking out of a salary plus commission role at a Fortune 500 company with no backup plan, a massive career shift to step into, and a number of steps in pursuit of that goal. It will spark one's Wild in ways that are necessary to grow, change, and become a better version of ourselves. Because doing a hard thing, especially one that we are afraid of setting out to do, always brings us one step closer to our Wild.

Moms and dads of young men of all ages, take note: You want your son to be just a little bit Wild. Trust me. Because as he gets older, it becomes far more difficult to infuse the Wild back into a boy who lacks it.

TIPS FOR GUYS

Reclaim your Wild by unplugging from technology, spending time in nature, building brotherhood, and embracing healthy, age-appropriate assertiveness to reduce passivity and anxiety.

Find your Wild—a challenge that pushes your limits. Compete with yourself and others to discover your true capacity and grow as a man.

Don't lose your Wild in the routine of life and the mundane of the day-to-day. Prioritize and protect time for what fuels your soul; it is essential for your wellbeing.

TIPS FOR PARENTS

Accept some age-appropriate acting out in boys and young men. It's easier to manage a boy's Wild early on than to try to restore it later.

Don't pathologize Wild. Physicality, aggressiveness, and restlessness can be natural traits of boys and seeds of qualities that can be celebrated in the future.

Dads, model Wild safely. Wrestle, camp, ski, box, and share stories—these moments teach your sons what it means to be a man.

LESSON 5

Never Tap Out

WE LIVE IN A WORLD where people quit quickly. More than 50 percent of marriages end in divorce. According to *USA Today,* 70 percent of athletes quit youth sports before they reach high school. In fact, we've become so adept at quitting as young men that we've even quit the act of quitting itself.

In the last few years, a relatively new phenomenon has emerged known as "quiet quitting," one in which we don't even care enough to exert the effort required to formally quit an activity. Instead, workers on the job exist by doing solely the minimum amount of work required to maintain their role. They work to intentionally curate the bare minimum effort and precisely thread that needle so as to not get fired while still maintaining their role. Without having the courage to admit it out loud, they have quit on themselves and their bosses and have quit demanding a reasonable performance. They are so disenchanted with the world around them, they have quit the process of quitting.

We men of all ages have also become quick to make excuses. In my business, diffusion of responsibility reigns. I recently had an 8:30 a.m. appointment with a young man. This was the second time we had officially booked after this nineteen-year-old had rescheduled with me on short notice. With this population, it often takes some time on the front end before I can get a kid in front of me, but when I do, I can usually get him to come back. Unfortunately, on this occasion, this kid straight up no-showed me. I texted him four times, Facetimed him three times, and called him twice. No response to any of those overtures.

Twenty minutes into the half hour, I reached out to his dad. Here is the message I shared:

"Hi Dad. Your son blew me off at 8:30 a.m. this morning. This is now the second time he's done so. I'll continue to work with you and your wife in an advisory capacity. But he's not ready to do the work."

Here was Dad's response:

"He just showed me his phone/texts … it's not showing any texts or calls from you … he claims to not have erased anything. Not sure what happened. I know your schedule is busy … can he Google meet with you? I'll have him send the link. LMK if you can make that work. Apologies for the confusion, not sure what's going on here."

I was less than stoked. My response reflected it:

"What's going on is he blew this appointment off, as he

often does with his commitments. Don't be an apologist for his lack of follow-through. In addition to me chasing him for the last four weeks and him being unresponsive, you're now communicating on his behalf and promoting his excuse making. I'm not willing to attempt to work with him directly any longer. We can revisit this down the line, depending on the type of effort we see from him on the home front going forward."

What bothered me the most was twofold: One, this parent, who was already inept at policing his son, implicitly questioned the legitimacy of my self-report. He immediately ran to the verbal aid of his son, corroborating his son's position and affirming his narrative. His knee-jerk reaction, rather than forcing his son to rectify the situation, was to assume there was an excuse to justify his son's behavior. He even questioned "what happened" when there was a single obvious answer.

Secondly, Dad quit being a dad. He quit holding his kid accountable. He quit demanding a basic level of respect from his son for other people, particularly those working to provide guidance and support. What makes matters worse is that this was a pro bono case. I'd been working for free, advising the parents and attempting to engage the son for the better part of six weeks as a favor to a close friend of mine. Not only was Dad unappreciative of the support he was receiving, but he didn't mandate that his kid move forward with receiving help he needed. In essence, Dad condoned his son quitting.

It's unfortunate, but with respect to our young men, we've quit having standards. We've allowed them to set goals and not follow through on them. We support their taking the easy way out.

Much of this comes from not wanting to see our boys unhappy. Establishing goals and achieving them for boys and young men is a patient game, and boys, especially now, live in a world of instant gratification. When they want a quick dopamine boost and need to feel better, they play the video games on their phones and in their bedrooms. When they desire the companionship of a female, they turn to porn to meet their physical impulse. When they seek relationship, they turn to online dating, which doesn't require consistency, patience, or an investment of one's resources. If they need to feed themselves, rather than going to the grocery store to prepare a healthy meal, they DoorDash food and spend $26 (including delivery fees and tip) on a grinder and a soda. It's a dangerous cycle.

As a result, young men lack patience, are allergic to delayed gratification, and struggle to plan and execute, particularly in the long term. Therefore, when they become frustrated, disappointed, or exhibit discontent, moms and dads find it easier to let their sons walk away than attempt to parent and hold them accountable. Truth is, walking away is easier, certainly in the short term. We don't have to deliver lectures, we don't have to communicate why our standards and attributes like work ethic, stick-to-itiveness, resilience, and keeping your word matter. Most young men aren't drawn to principles like these.

Thus, we find boys who walk off the field of play, out of the classroom, off the job, and into their bedrooms where they can grab a controller or phone and get lost in the noise of escapism by shutting the door behind them. In the short term, the allure of avoidance can be intoxicating.

But the message that persists when a young man quits begins to define the DNA of who they become. When a parent allows their son to quit, it communicates the following message to that young man: "Son, I'm okay with an unsatisfactory effort from you, and I'm okay with you being a lesser version of yourself than you have the capacity to be."

As a parent, it conveys that you are okay with your son making excuses for his behavior, that you are okay with him giving his word and not following through, and that, in general, any time he has the opportunity to do a hard thing, you will support him taking the easy way out. In general, we have supported young men lacking patience to sustain effort. And whether it is progress in the classroom, on the sports field, in the band room, or in relationships with family and friends, patience is a key ingredient for success. When you quit something, you lose the opportunity to practice patience and practice facing a hard thing and doing whatever is required to overcome it.

I have never been the smartest or the most educated, and I certainly have more limitations than strengths, but in the instances where I have achieved success in my life, the greatest common thread for me has been my unwillingness to quit, irrespective of the circumstances. Particularly in those moments, both at work and in my relationships, when things have been their bleakest, it has been my ability to "never tap out" that has delivered me through my darkest times.

For me, two of those moments reign supreme, one at work and the other at home. Both illustrate how embodying a "never tap out" approach to life allowed me to not only survive but eventually achieve an outcome I never could have imagined.

Take a look at yourself ...

According to data, as much as 40 percent of therapeutic outcomes are predicated upon the quality of the therapeutic alliance between the client and the therapist. Since I was as good at making relationships with highly defended, treatment-averse young men as anyone you'll ever meet, my baseline assumption was that I must be pretty good at relationships in general. At face value that tracked, as did the fact that I was married to a wonderful, beautiful, smart, kind, and hilarious woman—an objectively very cool person as well. One would assume if she was a reflection of me, then I must be pretty good at relationships in order to woo her enough to win her favor. And I had great kids, based upon the observations of my own lens as well as others' lenses, and we had seemingly good relationships, too.

Then life punched me in the face and forced me to take another look. Truth was, G and I were in a very bad place. We'd experienced years of the erosion that only time drifting can foster, built on a foundation of a fast-paced life, an ever-growing work empire, an overly busy schedule, and way too few collisions of substance in our life. I worked many hours. She worked a lot, too. But the more I worked, the more I wanted time together as a family unit and time for the two of us. The more I forced that interaction, the more she longed for the company of others to offset the pressure I applied. We were not okay.

For the ten years of my professional life prior to that realization, I believed in myself, having worked hard to come back from the abyss of my late teens and early twenties, conquering my demons along the way. I believed in my pride, my ability to overcome, my wealth, my smarts—anything I had cultivated as we built together a mini-fiefdom of self-importance. The trophies that sat on our mental mantle justified everything—the long nights; the yelling, screaming, snapping, swearing; and the raw, aggressive energy I relied on to build my business, expand my world, and save people. Now, none of that could save me from the depths of the mess I had made, the mess my marriage had become.

Back then, most of our issues stemmed from poor communication. In retrospect, I carried the brunt of that responsibility for a few reasons. Very quickly in our process of rebuilding our relationship, I did what most men are unable to do: I took personal responsibility. I looked back at our journey and saw the error of my ways. I even traced some of her acting out to some precipitants I believed were mine to own. In many ways, this was easy because Gina is a far more agreeable, far more delightful person than I at baseline. But in truth, had I not been able to raise my hand and take a look at myself, I don't believe we would have been successful in forging a path ahead.

It was easy to see where I was at fault and where I had led us astray. First, I was too defensive. I grew up in a household with frequent yelling and screaming. I internalized my mother berating my father on an almost daily basis, calling him names, belittling him, and using hurtful language that became customary for all of us to hear. So whenever I felt criticized by anyone—a teacher, a coach, my spouse—I could *feel* myself welling up inside. Becoming angry. Feeling attacked. Perceiving commentary that was intended as relatively benign as a massive affront. Gina found it virtually impossible to speak to me about matters of importance. My own historical exposures presented as a limiting factor to my ability to receive feedback and use it productively.

Second, I was very insecure. A major part of me still saw myself as both broken and undesirable, fully incapable of receiving love. My attachments to my parents were tenuous for much of my young adult life. In those early years of my marriage, I really didn't have relationships with either one of my folks (in the case of my mother, I still don't). But, in spite of accomplishing a lot professionally, marrying a wonderful woman, and having tremendous kids and great friends, I've always been a leaky bucket kind of guy: never full, never satisfied. Very much a posture and a mindset of lack. Upon reaching a goal, without ever celebrating my achievements, I would simply look to the horizon and fix my eyes on what was next. I was never appeased. Never comfortable.

I didn't trust people and was skeptical about relationships, motivation, and intentions, with the belief that many of the people closest to me had screwed me over and left me hanging out to dry. I assumed everybody would do the same. It made it hard for Gina to meet my needs as I always pushed and wanted more. I needed her reassurance, her encouragement, her affirmation. And so my insatiable desire for more of everything—sex, success, money, conquest, evidence that I was worthy—created an inability to be satisfied and to operate from a position of rest and peace.

Another insecurity, and potentially the most significant one, was directly related to my identity as someone who had a mental illness and was an addict. No single factor made me feel insecure in greater measure than those two labels. I felt forever marked by my bouts of depression and mania. I was scarred—physically, mentally, and emotionally—from a couple of inpatient hospitalizations. Many factors made me feel wholly inadequate: being in therapy for as long as I had and most likely requiring it for the rest of my life; taking medication as a crutch to manage my emotional issues; and self-identifying as an alcoholic in remission but with all the unhealthy codependent tendencies that characterize alcoholics.

Bottom came when the work began

By the end of 2017, the single relationship that mattered most to me—my marriage—was in shambles. When we finally stepped into couples counseling in early 2018, I had no concept of how bad it was. It was hard to hear that I was controlling, I didn't listen, I wasn't curious, I yelled a lot, I didn't make Gina feel safe, I didn't ask questions. I had a lot of pride in our marriage, and honestly, in who my wife was as a reflection of me. It was hard to even begin to understand the depths of how far I had drifted off course. That leveled me and encouraged me to begin asking questions, even if they weren't the right ones.

As I processed my role and my choices that contributed to the state of our life, I started sinking into a deep depression. I wasn't sleeping. I wasn't eating. My anxiety was worse than ever. I feared she was going to leave, that our family would be torn apart like my own, that my kids would suffer just as I had. Nearly all communication between me and G during that season was volatile, confrontational, and exhausting. I didn't have much else to give, and no matter how many people might have helped me and were willing to offer their support, it felt like I had no one. With all that I had built and all the people I had helped, I felt alone. I wasn't actively suicidal, but I definitely had thoughts of killing myself. I wished every day that God would make it stop and would end my suffering. This was my bottom.

The most challenging part, honestly, was in Gina communicating to me how much I had hurt her over the years. How much I had taken her for granted. How much I didn't share things with her—about work, about my thoughts. How little I cared for what she wanted or about what she thought, failing to be curious, ask questions, or be flexible in making decisions as a family. Because my life was so erratic at work, I craved routine, structure, and discipline at home. And in a season where she had a bunch of little kids, a big job, and way too little time and energy for herself, I demeaned her with incessant overtures for her attention. When I started understanding the scope of the problem and the weight of the emotional pain it caused her, I felt sick—not only because I had done that, but also because she didn't believe in me enough to share how impacted she was. She didn't believe in me enough to think I would have heard her or done anything with the information. Unfortunately, she was probably right.

Keep going

Many days, the pain felt like too much. Everything I had ever wanted—my marriage, my children, my business, my health—felt like it was slipping away. And it was. But as is often the case, it came down to two choices: I could stay and keep working, no matter the cost, or I could leave, tap out, and surrender my destiny to fate alone. Doing the work and not giving up felt like the only choice. But if I wanted to stay, I needed to dig in and commit myself to the work required to fix it. No matter how bad things became, I still loved her with all I had. Also, a part of me knew I couldn't find someone who understood me like she does and who has the capacity to love me in spite of all my messiness.

I also loved our unit. I loved my children. At that point, I couldn't imagine falling victim to divorce as my own folks had. I had pledged to myself years before that I was getting married once. I meant it. I promised myself not to let my kids suffer through what had plagued me and my siblings. I recognize that in many (if not most) situations of divorce, the process actually helps more than it hurts, particularly once a relationship falls apart. Call me a sucker or call me someone who just won't quit, but I wasn't going to surrender. Ever. Especially not with someone like Gina. I would be a fool.

And I sure would have been. Because as I sit here writing, there's a woman downstairs who is very much in love with me. That same woman was very much out of love with me seven years ago. Here's how I won her back:

1. I began to lead with yes

Many years ago, I half-jokingly said, "I'd rather have a rare disease than a swimming pool." I have a pool now. I quite like it. I also said, "Over my dead body will the Beneventos ever have a dog." I guess that's true, because now we don't have one—we have two. Back in the day, anything my wife and kids asked me was met with a curmudgeonly resistance. Pools and dogs required work, and because I was so overworked, I didn't have capacity and bandwidth to take care of things that felt like extras since I would most likely assume those responsibilities.

The challenge in our old marriage was that my "no" was

pervasive. I said no to people, to inviting people into our home, to pouring into and building relationships with others. I felt guilty about the lack of time I spent with G and the kids and became myopically focused upon maximizing the return on investment on that time with them on the weekends. But I wanted them all to myself, and I wanted us to be everything to each other. I excluded extended family and close friends. It frustrated G to no end. She wanted to expand the world of our family; I wanted to shrink it and maintain boundaries so I could have my wife and kids all to myself.

Now I see the innumerable benefits in cultivating rich, full, and selfless relationships by saying yes to the requests people make. Transformative experience comes from giving of our time in the form of true relationship. Few factors have been more important to transforming the culture of our home than my ability to lead with yes.

2. I became a whole person

I am somewhat embarrassed to say this, being a mental health professional for nearly twenty years, but the concept of personhood evaded me for my entire life until my couples work with G started a few years ago. Conceptually, I understood there are innumerable domains that constitute what it is to be a person, and that to be a full, balanced, and healthy individual, one must be strengthening those elements in a consistent and multidimensional way. Too much emphasis upon any one area causes deficits and holes in the others.

Because I was so myopically focused upon work and my immediate family, I not only lacked a sense of balance in my life, but I was unfulfilled. I didn't realize it, but I was dependent upon those other factors to provide me a sense of purpose and meaning. The more Gina's time and decisions were not her own and because she saw how hard I was trying and how depleted I was, she complied. But it took its toll.

Workwise, successes meant less and less the more frequent they became, and I lost touch with the value of the work, seeing it instead as just a job—one that took a lot out of me and was becoming more and more unsustainable and less enjoyable as we grew. For a while, and particularly coinciding with the emergence of critical issues in our relationship, what was mission-driven and once contained incredible purpose and nobility became something I resented. And if my marriage wasn't solid, and my relationships with my kids were distant, *and* I resented work, then who was I? And what did I have to feel good about?

If I wanted to save my family and my marriage, I needed to become a fuller, more balanced, more sustainable version of myself—primarily because I was on track to have a fatal heart attack by forty. I say that sincerely, by the way. In 2019, I was hospitalized overnight for chest pain, which although at the time was deemed nothing, most certainly would have materialized into something dangerous without significant shifts in my lifestyle. But I also needed to make changes because I wasn't showing up as a good version of myself. I was impatient. I was mean. I was cold. I valued the wrong things. Reprioritizing and reallocating my time, money, values, and approach to people allowed me to be more whole, and it helped me become a better partner to Gina and a better dad to my kids.

Being a whole person meant connecting to my interests. It meant finding things I enjoyed separate from my wife and children. It meant pulling back at work and reprioritizing some of that real estate from the work domain and putting it into places from which I derived more joy. Things that filled me. It meant exploring and finding my Wild again. It meant leaning into coaching, where I have been able to find a personal interest that became a passion. This interest also allowed me to pour back into my sons in new and profound ways as well.

But it also meant having friends. I was so busy at work and prioritized my life so much by being a provider and a mental health expert that I had very few meaningful relationships with other men. It meant identifying my deficits in this area but also leaning into a willingness to spend the time required to cultivate strong bonds with guys. (I'll dive into this more in the next lesson.) Healthy friendships have now become a bedrock of how I spend my time and how I have reprioritized my life.

Being a whole person means I can feel good, independent of others. My prior adult life was predicated upon who I was in relationship to my significant others, specifically in my role as husband and father. At thirty-five, I began to explore who I was independently of them, what I enjoyed doing, and how I could be successful in forming numerous and healthy relationships outside of my family unit.

3. I loved all of her

My wife is very, very easy to love. She's whip smart, incredibly kind, fun-loving, drop-dead gorgeous, funny, silly, sexy, and a high-character individual. I fell in love with her the first second I saw her seventeen years ago, and that sentiment has been a constant for the entirety of our relationship.

But I didn't love her well. I put my needs above hers. I didn't share space with her well. I wasn't curious about knowing her and knowing her heart. I applied pressure to do things my way, to live our lives my way, and to engage with the world through a lens that was comfortable for me. I liked privacy, quiet, and calm; she required the chaos only big families and big family dynamics can boast. She needed laughter, volume, and relationships with all their complexity. I wasn't flexible on those things, and it stifled Gina and pushed her farther away from me.

Truth was, I didn't really love all of her. You can only truly love someone well if you love all of them. Of course, I loved Gina when she was done up to the nines in pumps and a little black dress and we were out on the town. I loved her when she was telling me how amazing I was. I loved her when she was supporting me in running our business. In truth, I loved her when she met my needs.

But I didn't love her feedback. It offended me and made me feel small. I didn't love her ideas. They conflicted with my own and made me feel stupid. I didn't love her fully and completely when her grandmother was sick; it presented as an inconvenience for me and disrupted my plans and my routine. I didn't love her when she was sick in bed. I'm ashamed to say this, but it made me consider how long that would necessitate a sexual hiatus. I didn't love her when her clothes were tossed all over our bedroom floor. I felt disrespected. And I definitely didn't love her when her family was making decisions or prioritizing activities that frustrated me. I held her unduly accountable by extension and blamed her for not managing things well.

Loving someone is about loving all of that person. And it's the subtle imperfections—the underwear on the floor, the overbearing family dynamics, the forgetting to do things that one says they will—that allow us to appreciate how extraordinary the amazing parts truly are.

4. I prioritized serving her

For years, my own efforts were so front of mind that I couldn't appreciate the contributions Gina made every day. I was the one killing myself working harder than everyone else I knew, doing work that mattered more than everybody else's job. What I was doing was hard, and it needed to be celebrated.

Not only was that thinking highly flawed, but I felt it gave me license to opt out of everything else. Cleaning? We're making enough to have the cleaning lady come twice per week. No thanks. Taking care of the kids? Our nanny and my mother-in-law were on that. Doing kind little acts and functioning as a selfless and caring person? I didn't need to. I was a man on a mission; that mission was going swimmingly, and my ego was big as the horizon. She was the wife. I was the husband. She needed to serve me.

It was easy to see the flaws in that logic once it was spotlighted by both G and Lisa, our wizard of a couples therapist. The problem was, I didn't know how to shift it.

I found the answer in the most obvious of places: the Bible. Because I didn't know how to be humble, how to serve others, how to be selfless and put the needs of others in front of myself, I needed a framework to see the world through. To help me persevere when I became frustrated. To motivate me that my efforts were oriented in the right direction.

In the book of Ephesians, the Apostle Paul tells the church,

"Husbands, love your wives, just as Christ loved the church and gave himself up for her. … In this same way, husbands ought to love their wives as their own bodies. He who loves his wife loves himself" (Ephesians 5:25–29). Ironically, it doesn't instruct wives to love their husbands; they're already hardwired to do so, but it seems as though we husbands need the reminder.

Paul speaks directly to the biblical encouragement for men to be Christlike in their approach to their spouse. Jesus died for the church and for his followers—really for the world, including his non-followers. In commanding us to do the same as men, Paul is instructing men to die to self, to elevate their wives in front of them. This doesn't mean a physical death nor does it mean killing all strength, ambition, courage, or value for men. Rather, it's a repositioning of objective. The goal now, for me, is to put my wife above myself in any and all matters, and serve her first for the good of our home and our relationship. It is to prioritize her needs over my own. It is the decision by a man, consciously, to bury his own self-importance, grandiosity, and needs and raise his wife over himself. It means, for us as men, the desire to surrender all that we have in their name and in the name of our love for them. Those ideas, as expansive and impossible to attain as they may seem, gave me a point on the bullseye to aim for. It was a wonderful place to start.

This led to me doing things that had evaded me for years, like bringing her coffee in bed every morning to start the day, with just a kiss on the forehead and an "I love you." Leaving notes telling her I appreciate her. Taking time off from work to do house projects alongside her that had been piling up for years—not because she needs my help (she's much handier than I) but just because they matter to her. Listening to her.

Accepting her feedback. Validating her perspective. Caring about her wants.

I began to operate in life by examining things through a lens of "How can I best serve G today, and what are the ways I can help her feel most loved and most seen?" It was highly imperfect in terms of implementation, and I required her correction often because I frequently overdid it (given that I mostly overdid everything). However, the shift helped reprioritize my focus and allowed her to see the depth of my affection for her in an earnest way.

Ironically, now seven-plus years later in our own process of rebuilding our relationship, this shift in ideology has reciprocally led to my wife willingly reprioritizing my needs in front of her own. But I had to lead that shift, and I had to demonstrate my authenticity in doing so in order for her to trust me and step inward in kind.

The other side

Today, I sit on the other side of that work with my wife. It was five years of knock-down drag-outs and many days of three steps forward, one step back, followed by two years of healing and reestablishing a new normal. For me, there was never a decision as to whether I should stay or leave.

I wish I could say the work was easy. It wasn't. It was the hardest thing I have ever done. I desperately hope that the sum total of our effort positions my wife and me to avoid ever undertaking a painstaking process like this again. Either way, these steps, which are simple to understand but difficult to implement, helped shift the framework in our relationship in many ways: saying "no" almost exclusively to being open to most things; being unbalanced to seeking balance; being all about me to focusing on Gina. Selfish to selfless. Me first to her first. Loving myself and serving my own needs to loving all of her and serving her with my first fruits.

This is the world we live in now.

But only because the two of us agreed to never tap out. Ever.

The Case of Stevey

I REMEMBER when Stevey came to see me for the first time. He was just a little guy, probably thirteen at the time. I could see the pain behind his blank stare. He would drop his gaze when he spoke to me, frequently breaking eye contact. He was handsome and small in stature but lean and wiry. His olive complexion gave way to deep brown eyes and a puff of wavy hair on top. It was easy to see why the girls liked him. He had that laid-back, lax bro vibe about his countenance that people seemed to find disarming.

His parents were small in stature too. Dad was an Ivy League—educated CEO of a large publicly traded company. He was kind, soft spoken, and patient, and he loved his son a great deal. Dad was willing to do whatever was required to help his son get well. He was a good participant in the treatment process. Dad was the glue that helped hold the family together when things got hard for those years.

Mom was an anxious mess but easy to love. She had a

huge, bubbly, gregarious personality, big curly hair that she wore blown out or in a mane of curls. She was well connected in the local community, had a million friends, and was popular with the moms in Stevey's peer group. But when Stevey's best friend died in a tragic skiing accident, his entire family system blew up.

Devastating

The accident was a massive hit to the entire community and a public loss for all. The grieving consumed the entire eighth grade class that lost their beloved shining star, JT, but no one was hit as hard as Stevey, who was there when it happened.

The two boys were shredding the mountain, side by side as they always were. JT hit a tree, and Stevey saw it happen. He immediately planted, carved, jumped out of his skis, and hurried back up the hill, where he found his best friend bleeding profusely from his head and face. JT gasped for breath and made sounds that Stevey would later recount for me as we scripted his trauma narrative. Stevey actually ripped his own shirt off right on the slopes and wrapped it around his buddy's skull to try to hold his best friend's head intact. Unfortunately, it was far too late. JT was dead by the time they got him off the mountain. In fact, he took his last breath in Stevey's arms.

The devastating loss had a major impact on the community. I remember one of the high school counselors talking about how this group of boys came together to process their respective trauma. One of the parents, who went to pick up seven or eight of the boys at school where they were all hanging out about a week after the accident, found the group near the playground, lying on top of each other like a litter of puppies, cuddling and seeking comfort from one another. For most boys that age, parents would consider that bizarre behavior. From my perspective, it was a collective trauma response to a deep wound that all the boys shared, down to their core.

Beyond broken

By the time he showed up in my office, Stevey was beyond broken. He was rageful. He attacked his father. He had night terrors. He stopped going to school almost completely. He was banging his head incessantly against the hardwood floors in his house, trying desperately to make himself feel anything. He destroyed walls and property almost daily. He was decompensating quickly, deteriorating in his mental condition a little bit more every day. He was struggling to feel things in an appropriate way, but to a greater degree, he was struggling to feel at all. This was how the rest of eighth grade went.

By the time Stevey got to high school, he couldn't sleep, and he was having recurring thoughts of hurting himself. Even more frequently, he was making threats about hurting others, specifically his parents, and becoming violent on almost a daily basis. The saddest part of all was that prior to the trauma, Stevey had never demonstrated any violent or aggressive characteristics.

The decompensation continued to crescendo upward, and despite my best efforts as his therapist to keep him well, nothing we were doing in therapy was really working. Yes, we had a great relationship. And yes, because of that, he was most certainly trying. He would come to sessions prepared, do the work in session, and complete whatever homework I gave him. We talked about the future, his goals, ways to manage his mood, factors that could help him manage his sleep, and his aggressive tendencies. But none of these conversations or the attempts to acquire any useful skills mattered. The smallest hairpin trigger at home would almost immediately cause him to explode. Mom was just working to hold him accountable and trying to do her best, but he would become rageful any time she said anything he didn't like.

But even in his worst moments, Mom refused to tap out, choosing instead to receive his onslaught, no matter how intense or targeted. Dad, equally committed to his broken boy, also refused to tap out in any way. This typically manifested itself as him forcibly restraining his son to prevent Stevey from seriously injuring himself for as long as was required until he would wear himself out and fall asleep. But Stevey was getting older and growing stronger. We knew this was an unsustainable path for the family, regardless of their commitment to their son and their willingness not to quit.

We needed to up the ante as a collective.

It all blew up

I went to the house to do a home visit one night, and that was when it all blew up. It was 6:35 p.m. on a Tuesday when I arrived. The space itself was incredible. Though the house looked somewhat modest on the outside and had an energy that felt cozy when you walked in, the interior revealed not only an impeccable design but a sprawling open floor plan. I opened the double French doors in the foyer to reveal one of the largest kitchens I've ever seen, almost a thousand square feet, with twenty-foot cathedral ceilings, a large brick double inlay fireplace, and floor-to-ceiling cabinets on all three walls that took my breath away. But it was impossible to focus on the otherworldly aesthetic with the active danger unfolding in front of me. When I got there, they were all in the kitchen, and Stevey was already activated, yelling and screaming at his parents.

Stevey was standing directly in front of me while his parents sat next to him, one on each side. He was both angry and animated, and a vein pulsed in his neck as he spoke.

"Fuck you both. I fucking hate you. I hope you both fucking die!" he screamed.

I responded immediately in a voice soft enough to be called a whisper as I put my right hand on his shoulder. "Bro … I know you don't mean that."

He calmed down for a second. I assumed he was done and would take a seat. But he started walking backward toward the fireplace against the back wall of the kitchen. I interpreted this as his best effort to take some physical space, and so I didn't feel the need to intercede. But as his mom tried to de-escalate the situation, only further agitating him, he ripped the biggest knife out of the nearby butcher block and held it to his throat. She shrieked and fell to the floor, screaming and crying. Dad raised his hand but couldn't get a word out.

I immediately stepped right in the middle of the three of them, the knife still pressed fully against the young boy's neckline.

As calmly as I have ever articulated any sentence in my life, I firmly but gently spoke to him: "Stevey … come with me outside to get a breath. But first, you need to put the knife down."

He clutched it tight and looked me in the eyes, with tears in his own. But he wouldn't let it go. As he had done so many times in my office, he dropped his gaze. The knife remained firmly in his grasp.

I took another large step toward him, making sure my eyes were fixed on him the entire way. I gently put my hand on his shoulder again. "Stevey. Give me that." He finally did. And together we walked outside.

I knew what I had to do

While we were outside, I knew what I had to do. I needed to somehow choreograph the 911 call. This kid wasn't safe and needed to be in a hospital. Otherwise it was just a matter of time before something very bad happened.

About fifteen minutes later, when he was settled and I had the knife in my possession, I went back inside. He was safe enough to leave alone by this point, at least for a brief second while I communicated with his folks. I told them to call 911 immediately, and that I was going back outside to make sure he was safe. I directed them to communicate to the dispatch officer that their son was unruly and out of control, but police presence would make him escalate further. As a result, the cops and EMTs needed to park at the end of the driveway and walk up, at least initially, to not raise his ire after I'd calmed him down. They listened. I also instructed his parents to communicate to their son when the next steps began unfolding that *they* had called 911, not me. I would be intimately involved in the next steps to help keep him calm since I had earned his trust.

I was good to my word

When the cops arrived, Stevey lost his composure again. Fortunately, I was again successful in helping him to gather himself. I reinforced to him that everything would be okay, I would be with him the entire way, I would never quit on him, and the best thing he could do was to be calm and follow the first responders' instructions. He said he would only go to the hospital if I came with him in the ambulance and if I stayed with him there.

I was good to my word.

I took the ride over in the ambulance with Stevey to the nearest hospital emergency room. He was there for thirty-six hours. I was there for nearly the entire time, leaving just twice to go home and sleep for four hours and shower, only to come back and sit with him and his family and wait for next steps. Eventually, we found a bed for Stevey at a local treatment center, where he went directly from the hospital. I visited him four times during the seventy-five-day stay. When he was discharged to our care, we picked right back up, this time with a different degree of focus and specificity about the road forward. Never deterred, always committed, never willing to tap out. Stevey. His parents. And me.

Different work

By the time that he got back from his stay in treatment, the world looked very different. Stevey had accepted his diagnosis of PTSD and was willing to take medication to help manage the symptoms. He accepted the need for medication to help manage his angry and aggressive outbursts. He understood it might not be the case forever, but he knew it was required for the foreseeable future. As a result, Stevey was regulated, having personally experienced the benefits that an inpatient stay can have on identifying, modifying, and eventually calibrating the ideal regimen to manage his mood. His outbursts slowed to a virtually nonexistent frequency. He was calm and able to articulate his feelings much better, having gone through far more intensive therapy than he ever could have done with me in an outpatient framework.

He was in a much better place, and seeing gains made him feel motivated and far more secure. But he had to work through the depths of his trauma, not being able to get much past the efforts to solidify his mood in the initial phase of treatment. Now, the stage was set for the real work to occur for Stevey.

Upon discharge, Stevey started working simultaneously with our lead psychologist as well, who was phenomenal in rendering highly structured, manualized Cognitive Behavioral Therapy (CBT) in which the therapist looks to reframe irrational thoughts and tie those reframed thoughts to a change in behavior, which drives a subsequent change in emotional response.

Using this framework, our psychologist developed a graduated exposure hierarchy to create common language about the situation Stevey had faced in his past. They examined the emotions he was feeling from the trauma he endured as he recounted those moments unfolding in real time. They examined the severity of Stevey's anxious responses to those feelings. They talked about specific behaviors he could engage in to cope with his symptoms when he started to experience distress again. This rational, common-sense approach helped elevate Stevey to a different degree of understanding concerning the depths of his pain.

Once he had the language to better describe what he was feeling, Stevey began to develop an understanding of how broken he was because of the accident. He and our psychologist physically ventured out into the community, starting with places Stevey and JT used to hang out, progressing to the area in proximity to the accident. Slowly and gradually, through the trust of a supportive therapist, Stevey was able to visit the site of the accident itself, speak fluidly about his emotions, offer a well-adjusted emotional response to what he was experiencing, and manage his emotions within an appropriate range. This demonstrated that he had started to accept the loss.

Treating the root cause

From there, I leveraged my long-standing relationship with Stevey to work alongside the exposure therapy process and simultaneously help him craft a trauma narrative. In doing so, he wrote extensively, precisely, and powerfully about his pain and the moments surrounding the accident. How JT looked and sounded as he lay in the snow. How much blood was at the scene. How he responded to seeing JT's parents for the first time after the accident. What he remembered from the funeral. The narrative process helped Stevey purge the bottled-up emotions that had once haunted his nightmares.

It certainly wasn't a straight line for Stevey. In fact, it was nearly two years of work before he was fully discharged from our care if you count the initial period prior to his hospitalization as well as his time inpatient. But our work was an opportunity for him to put his feet on the ground and move forward. The active work he did in therapy enabled him to move toward a better version of his future. Once he arrived at a better place, Stevey came to terms with the fact that the accident wasn't his parents' fault nor was it their responsibility to fix. His mom was able to recognize that it was Stevey's situation to heal from; she didn't have to assume his burdens all on her own. Dad was able to take a firmer position with Stevey, whereas previously he had used kid gloves because his boy was so deeply wounded and fragile, and Dad was so fearful he would hurt himself or someone else.

Before the family system could heal, we needed to treat not only the symptoms but the root cause. The unresolved trauma, as soon as it was effectively addressed and worked through, paved the way for this young man to step forward into the next phase of his life. He finished high school with great grades and went on to go to an Ivy League school. Stevey, by the end of his collective tenure with Causeway, with all of its phases, learned to accept himself.

Years ago, your dad saved my life

Not long ago, I took my sons and their two buddies to a Celtics game at The Boston Garden. From across the concourse, I heard a man yell, "Vince!" I turned and saw Stevey sprinting toward me. He told me he'd graduated from Penn a couple years before, and he lives in the city with his girl. He has been working in sports media for the last few years. He told me he is genuinely happy and healthy. He looked incredible: handsome, muscular, well-groomed. Filled with pride.

He shook hands with my boys and said to them, "My name is Stevey, and years ago your dad saved my life."

Stevey was only able to move forward in his life after reconciling his unresolved trauma, which was the result of a horrific childhood loss, and reaching a place of both knowledge and self-acceptance.

He worked with a team of therapists at Causeway, one an expert clinician who moved him through an exposure ladder to visit the accident site in a graduated way; the other, myself, who intervened in his kitchen, de-escalated him in a life-threatening circumstance, and then painstakingly assisted in developing Stevey's trauma narrative, allowing a release valve for his pain.

Through it all, I saw parents who never quit on their son, and a young man who never quit on himself. I saw their pain in watching their son suffer in overwhelming ways. I saw him, and them, nearly quit on many occasions and watched time and again Stevey's parents' perseverance reveal itself in the form of unending love for their son. Stevey's family relied on bountiful love to unify them and move them through their lowest moments. Through their love, they afforded Stevey enough room to eventually arrive at a place of peace.

Today it's okay

The world tells us today it's okay to quit. Daily. When something isn't going our way, it has become commonplace for people to turn their backs on a hard situation and walk away; we view that decision as the rule and not the exception. We expect to see people give up now when things get hard, frankly, because that is what men do.

We see it with men and specifically young men. We see

rates of college success at all-time lows for men, with nearly two-thirds of college students identifying as women, compared with roughly 40 percent some fifty years ago. Not only are women outperforming their male counterparts, but men are quitting school at an alarming frequency.

But, the alarming trend doesn't end with items that are impermanent; young people are quitting in escalating measure where the stakes are finite.

According to the National Institutes of Health, the suicide rate among men in 2022 was four times higher than that of women. But potentially even more alarmingly, rates of suicide have increased dramatically for both genders in the last five to ten years. According to the Jed Foundation, 22 percent of high school students reported having seriously considered suicide in the past year. These escalated numbers can trace their roots to 2009, when social media became broadly available on mobile devices, leading to an escalation in bullying, and specifically cyberbullying.

I have come close

I've said a few times in this lesson that I just don't quit. However, I have come close. So did Stevey. At age nineteen, I was hospitalized for having thoughts of ending my life. At age thirty-five, with my marriage on the rocks, my wife professing that our marriage was broken, and questioning whether we would have a successful future together, I experienced increasing mental health symptoms. I often thought people would be better off without me, that it would be far easier if I didn't exist. At that time, I couldn't envision another way out.

There have been days when I thought my family would be better off without me. There were days where Stevey felt the same way—for him, there was no hope; he didn't matter. He wouldn't be missed.

But when I was at my lowest, I held on tight to the people who love me. No matter how I felt about them at that moment, I thought of how they would be impacted if I gave up. I clung hard to hope for what my life could be—an image of my family, filled with joy, and my relationship with my wife, where we were connected and peaceful, our issues a distant memory. I thought of my kids and their limited access to their father, where they would see me only on weekends or potentially not at all. On the opposite side, I saw a hope-filled narrative where I was coaching games, cheering on the sidelines, or watching my baby girl dance while I held her mother's hand. These images, in some ways far-reaching possibilities, pushed me forward when tapping out felt like inches away.

As a young man in a psychiatric hospital, I never gave up on my vision for my life, even though there were times when I desperately wanted to. Even as a guy who was no longer at college and was the farthest thing from a productive member of society, I refused to accept defeat. Anything short of death itself, I recognized, could be changed, improved, or in some ways completely redefined.

Stevey knew it, too. No matter how much pain he suffered, whether he was at residential treatment or strapped to a gurney at the hospital, he continued to believe his fate was still yet to be determined. For Stevey, seeing his parents and me standing next to him the entire time proved to him that he had worth and value.

Share these stories

When you're in front of someone who wants to tap out, share these true stories to demonstrate that they always have an ability to change their outcome.

Tell them about the nineteen-year-old who wanted to end his life but didn't and who went on to change the way that therapy is done with young men, some twenty-five years later, because he never quit on himself, no matter how close he came.

Tell them about the fourteen-year-old who held a knife to his neck in his kitchen who later became an Ivy League—educated sports media mogul. Tell them that young man never stopped working until he fixed his pain after suffering a tragic loss.

Tell them about the thirty-five-year-old business owner and successful therapist who almost lost his marriage and his family as a result of prioritizing the wrong things. Remind them that same guy has a woman who truly loves him standing by his side and the most beautiful family you've ever seen living in a home filled with love.

Find someone who is about to tap out. Convince them not to. Because they are worth it. Because life is worth it. Because their vision for their life is still yet to be determined, so long as they don't quit.

TIPS FOR GUYS

Perseverance matters more than talent, charm, or experience—especially in situations of adversity. As long as you keep going, success remains possible.

There's value in effort, even without success. Failure can teach more than winning—through experience, discipline, and growth, you can still move forward.

Grit grows by not quitting. Sticking with hard things builds resilience, toughness, and persistence over time.

TIPS FOR PARENTS

Always prioritize safety. If someone shows signs of self-harm—even subtle ones—act decisively. In Stevey's case, we were cautious about retraumatizing him, but his safety came first. When in doubt, call 911. Nothing else matters more than making sure someone is safe.

As a parent, never tap out. Divorce can be the right choice in some cases, but fighting for your marriage and family should come first. If you're not willing to give your all here, what will you fight for? These are battles worth your full effort.

Don't settle in your marriage. My wife and I went from disconnection to deep friendship by committing to growth. With honesty, effort, and self-reflection from both sides, a struggling relationship can transform into something stronger than you could have ever imagined.

LESSON 6

Iron Sharpens Iron: Men Require Relationship

The absence of male relationship

FOR MEN, the idea of cultivating relationship is confusing. In many ways, male relationship is actually un-American. Since the times of pioneers on the American frontier, the American male has subscribed to both a culture of rugged individualism and a canon of male icons representing that ethos in both name and optics. Teddy Roosevelt.

John Wayne. Clint Eastwood. Sylvester Stallone. Even more recently, Kevin Costner's portrayal of John Dutton in *Yellowstone*. These symbols of folklore, masculinity, and male behavior silently preach qualities of being a man that we implicitly seek to embody. Stoicism. Protection. Self-reliance. Independence. Quick thinking and problem-solving. Never showing weakness. These attributes have been woven into the fabric of what it means to be a man in American society, particularly one who can be admired.

But within that framework stands a glaring omission: male companionship and relationship. In the iconic examples of what it is to be a man, we don't see guys who are hanging out with other men or seeking their company. We don't see men who are social, who lean on one another to meet their emotional needs and fill their cup. And we certainly don't see male icons of masculinity who ask for help and have an ability to be vulnerable in pursuit of support for other men. As a result, we lack images, symbols, or examples from our historical heroes' conduct that show us how to be men who have relationships with other men.

After doing work with men and young men for twenty years, I can attest to the notion that men and young men have problems developing and maintaining relationships. They don't know how to communicate well, particularly about their feelings. They find it difficult to venture away from conventional notions of success and toward mining their interests and pursuing their passions with all they have. As a result, they lack rich experiences to share within the context of relationship.

To some, the idea that men struggle in their relationships with women is most certainly not a surprise. Over the past half decade, it's been made abundantly clear that some men, particularly white men, engage in problematic relationship behavior. Some men, particularly affluent white men, have given almost all men a bad name by the way they treat women, propagate misogyny, degrade and belittle others, verbally, physically, and emotionally abuse others, and generally engage in conduct that makes men as a species look terrible.

But what may be a surprise is not how bad men are at developing relationships with women; it's how bad they are at developing relationships with each other. The most constant refrain I hear from young men is regarding the absence of relationship with other young men. The US Surgeon General stepped forward in 2023 and identified that one of the most serious and widespread health threats facing Americans today isn't drugs, depression, or violence—it's loneliness. Our inability to make friends as men and cultivate meaningful relationships with peers has led to a generation of empty, disconnected, emotionally inept, dissatisfied men and young men.

As a result of the absence of inputs, men and young men glean information about relationships from a variety of sources, making it difficult in our culture to understand what to do and how to be. We hear oral tradition stories of guys who are affirmed for being sexually active at early ages. In media and pop culture, we see athletes, actors, rappers, and rock front men who are lauded for their sexual conquests with beautiful women. We watch movies about guys who have star-crossed connections with women on first dates, and we long for that kind of spark, which is rarely present in reality. The trouble is, depending on where you grab those inputs, incoming information often doesn't fit, sources conflict, and it becomes confusing and noisy to determine what's most important and what to hold most dear. Thus, it's hard for men to know how to treat a woman and what is most important in doing so.

The only way

The only way for men to both be and do better is in the presence of other men. Proverbs 27:17 tells us that "as iron sharpens iron, so one person sharpens another." At Causeway, we have seen this principle unfold thousands of times in the past fourteen years. We believe through the direction, accountability, support, compassion, and communication around identification of better alternatives, a young man can shape his behavior in the presence of another man and find life-changing support.

In sharing our burdens with another man, we can find answers that have been illuminated through the wisdom of another's experience. In receiving emotional support, we can identify that even in the midst of our lowest moments, we are not alone. When we are acting out, as men so often do, the sharpening that can only come through another man's accountability can redirect us toward a better decision and back onto a path that can help us feel proud. Dull men make careless mistakes and engage in shameful behavior. Dull men forget what they have at stake. Dull men tap out.

The same spot

As a successful therapist in my mid-thirties, I found myself in the same spot as most other men. The painful truth, which I learned after I finally got over my reservations and sought out my own therapy, was that even at my age, I had never matured in my ability to develop relationships. Real relationships. As a grown man in the prime of my career, with more money than I ever thought I would see, I accepted the fact that I sucked at relationships. And I had no real friend with whom I experienced authentic bonds.

At that time, I wasn't even able to enjoy my own family to the best of my ability, let alone make room for new friends, largely because the commitments in the work domain felt so colossal. To me, relationships were secondary, and even the ones I was invested in—my wife and kids—didn't receive the time, energy, and attention they deserved.

When I attempted to have relationships with friends, I realized that my friendships, for my entire life, had been mostly transactional in nature. When I needed something, I would call a friend. When they needed something, they would call me. My brother-in-law called me to help him move when he bought a new house; I called him when I needed some manpower when we moved about eight years ago. When another friend needed help building a swing set for his boys, I showed up to help him move lumber and lend a hand holding things while he did the assembly (as you might recall, I'm not super handy). As such, I called upon him when it was time to build our new grill one summer when we foolishly didn't elect to have it put together in-store. In those dyads, I did most of the talking and consumed most of the space in the room as I held court, demanding a lot of the energy that others possessed.

Hiding in plain sight

For me, genuinely, relationships were mostly about getting my needs met. At that time, my needs consisted of working, providing, and supporting my family in the very rudimentary manner I conceptualized. Either way, it wasn't about fun. I didn't have much joy in my friendships and didn't have any personal areas of interest outside of work, where I could meet new guys and make friends. I didn't have my own hobbies and didn't take care of myself in any meaningful way. As a kid, I loved sports, video games, and playing with action figures, but as a man, I didn't give myself room to play, largely because I felt it was wasteful and limited my ability to earn, which was my primary job.

As an adult, Gina made it easier for me to hide in plain sight, as women often do for their less-than-social husbands. Since so much of my time was in the work domain, she took any and all responsibility for our social calendar, making plans for us as a couple and for our family every weekend. We'd have couples over—those who had kids at least—on Friday nights, so we could have some time to relax while the kids played. On Saturdays, we'd have the kids' sports and activities during the daytime and then do a family activity in the evening, like grabbing dinner at a pizza joint or going to Nonni's to watch a movie as a family for as long as G and I could keep our eyes open. I was simply along for the ride, mostly as a holdover in between hitting my next work assignment so I could pick up where I left off, cookin' with gas at a hundred miles an hour. I wasn't invested in people. I was far more invested in my work, limited in my ability to be warm and caring with others, and desiring privacy and peace as a function of my need to reload for the next day. I couldn't be bothered.

On the opposite side of a couch

It all started in church one Sunday. Back then, as was often the case, I was trying to get in and out of there as quickly as possible. At that point, G was working, still taking classes in the city in pursuit of her master's degree, and she was pregnant with our first son, Vincey. As such, she got just about anything she wanted.

That Sunday in question, an older man in the congregation got up and asked for assistance in moving across town the following Saturday. G looked at me with the power of an infrared laser, seemingly motivated by her desire to leverage her influence. She used her eyeballs to inform me not so gently that it would be nice for me to help this gentleman. Nonverbal message received.

It was a typical day of moving heavy things stemming from my wife voluntelling me to help that gentleman. Assisting in the form of physical labor happened to be something I have a decent amount of experience with, as a guy who's both in shape and not handy. As the day drew to a close, I found myself squared up on opposite ends of an oversized loveseat with a guy about my age.

"Hey, dude. I'm Vinny." (Vinny is both my non-work name

in social spheres as well as the label I used in high school. I shed it quickly when I met G, however, as her brother's name is Vinny, which he prefers to go by. As a result, she strongly preferred I did not).

"Nice to meet you. I'm Ty."

Come to find out, Ty's wife was expecting too. Vincey was due any day, and they were just a couple of months along with a baby themselves.

"So how are you feeling about things?" he asked, attempting to make small talk about our pregnancy. I'm sure he didn't expect the answer he received.

"I'm petrified," I told him, and proceeded to list the litany of reasons why I felt myself unqualified for being a reasonably good father and husband. What if he would have a mental illness, like me? What if he would wrestle with addiction for most of his life, like me? What if he would suffer trauma like me? What if he had a broken relationship with his dad, like I did with mine, for much of my life? Ty and I hit it off rather well as a result of my candor, and I had never had a friend from church before.

But it was more than just my candor. I availed myself to this man I didn't even know. My vulnerability allowed for connection. It created a relational fabric that was ripe for common ground; my sharing allowed Ty to let his guard down, too. I led the way in helping my new acquaintance observe that he wasn't the only one with those same questions. My disclosure fostered shared experience. Thus, the friendship started. As G does, she invited them over a week or two later.

So why was this so unique? What is it about vulnerability that makes it so difficult for men, especially when in the company of one another? For one thing, vulnerability is socially constructed as an attribute commonly associated with weakness. The conventional icons of masculinity—those we see in movies, music, and culture—rarely emote, rarely convey they are in need of help, and even less frequently seek the help of another man. To seek help is to be weak. Sharing our concerns and anxieties with another man shows that we don't have what it takes, in whatever situation we find ourselves. As men, we pride ourselves upon our ability to be independent, solve problems without aid, and help and care for those around us. Demonstrating vulnerability calls our individualism into question, fueling the notion that we may, in fact, be dependent on someone else. Dependency is the opposite of what is conventionally masculine, which instead hinges upon the conventional belief that a man is an island unto himself.

But, in truth, isn't mastery of the self about not having secrets? Isn't integrity—what I regard as the truest measure of a man—about knowing oneself thoroughly and representing that singular version of self in all the different domains of one's life? After twenty-plus years of therapy, and nearly twenty years of working to serve the needs of men and young men, I believe one thing is undoubtedly true: Only in our vulnerability can we find our greatest strength. Only in our weakness can we find the depth of our pain and work through it en route to wholeness and healing. As men, only by availing ourselves to another can we shape who we are and be held to a standard we cannot achieve in isolation. When we are fully transparent and fully known, what is there to hide?

This is the power that only vulnerability can bring to a man's life.

The next ten years

For the next ten years, we did life with our new friends. We went to church together every week; we went over to their house every Sunday after church or grabbed lunch together when we were pressed for time. We raised our kids alongside one another, basically having children in an alternating framework every six months for the better part of four years. We vacationed together. We immersed ourselves into their family's annual summer pilgrimage to Hampton Beach, New Hampshire, where Ty and his family had vacationed for thirty-eight consecutive Memorial Days. We spent many holidays together. We would find our way to their Thanksgiving table for dessert on an annual basis and even shared the sacred July 4 celebrations that doubled as their eldest daughter's birthday. We held babies. Went to funerals. I was in the hospital room holding his mother's hand on the day she took her last breath.

We cried. Laughed. Started a business together—a small real estate holding company that allowed us to buy property together. We later dissolved that same business without damage to our relationship. Birthdays. Sports. Weddings. Parties. Hospital beds. We did life, in its highest and lowest forms, across all four seasons as a unit. Together for more than a decade.

He was there

And so, in the depths of my lowest, most fragile, most susceptible point, my best friend Ty was there. When Gina and

I were fighting for our marriage with all that we had, he was there. When I lost fifteen pounds and couldn't eat or sleep for days on end, he was there. When I was angry that despite battling depression with all I had, things only continued to get worse, he was there. When I was actively experiencing suicidal ideation—when I would drive to and from work every day, contemplating whether I should drive my car into the median at high speed—he was there. True, he was my only friend at the time, but he was most certainly there. Whether I asked or not, in fact, he was there.

One morning, things were particularly bad between me and Gina. I hadn't slept in days and was sick, barely able to speak, as my depression had an overwhelming stranglehold on me. I was still actively working, but outside of that, G and I were barely on speaking terms, and I didn't have much energy to engage with the kids in my waking hours outside of work. My psychiatrist and I were working aggressively to adjust my cocktail of meds, but we were finding little success in providing relief. The sleep aids and mood stabilizers I was prescribed weren't working. My pain was bordering on desperation.

Every part of me

One day, in the midst of the fog that was my life at the time, I came out of a session to find my best friend Ty sitting in my lobby.

"What are you doing here?" I curtly asked.

"I just came to see my friend," he said.

Every part of me wanted to kick him out of my office

as my broken pride welled up, even in one of my lowest moments. However, my wits, in conjunction with an absence of any physical energy at all, necessitated that I merely follow him.

"Get in," he commanded firmly as we stood outside his black F-150, which he still has to this day. I listened.

And we sat. We didn't speak much. I cried a bit, and so did he. He was burdened by the pain he saw his friend sitting in and felt my frustration at the lack of progress I was making. But he just told me that he loved me, and that I would figure it out, and G and I would figure it out. That if I just kept faith, kept believing things would get better, and did what I could every day to simply "do the next right thing," things would eventually be better.

I didn't believe him, and honestly, at that moment, I was angry—angry I was in that position. Angry things were so hard for me. Angry that despite battling depression and suicidal ideation and insomnia for months, things only continued to get worse. Which is precisely why, regardless of whether I wanted him to be there or not, he was there. When I was too depressed to speak, when I didn't have words to share, when all I could do was pick up the phone and cry, he listened and was there.

Not a therapist. Not my wife. Not my kids.

Another man. Fighting alongside me. Carrying the burden with me.

"I'm going to be here with you. Every day. Until you get through this," my best friend promised. And I can assure you he was good to his word.

Being authentic

Ty showed me the necessity of men being authentic with other men. Never before in my life had I been forced to be so brutally honest about how bad things were, how embarrassed I was, how small a degree of self-belief I could muster. Never before had I shared my weakness with another man, nor had I admitted to myself, let alone someone else, that I couldn't manage the situation alone. Never before had I cried and hugged and held another man, allowed him to feel my pain and sit with me in it. But in doing so—in communicating all those things—I had someone there next to me in my despair. My sole friendship became, in my lowest moment, a beacon that instilled in me what the best of relationships could offer.

My interactions with Ty and the genuine friendship that developed changed the way I defined male relationships. Prior to that, I saw myself as self-important and independent by nature, and I did not require another man to support me as I moved through life. I felt capable in my own power, valued privacy over disclosure, and leaned more heavily on myself than others. Since then and forever thereafter, I see that men require relationship with other men. That male companionship allows us to accomplish more as a collective than we could ever do in isolation. I would have most likely tapped out on working to fix my marriage if I did not have someone cheering for me, supporting me, and holding me to account to ensure I became a better version of myself along the way. Absent that support and care, I would have most definitely drifted into poor decision-making, relapse, or worse.

The standard Ty held for me and set alongside me helped

me believe in a better version of myself even when I wasn't in the headspace to demand that version of myself. Constant check-ins gave me energy when I didn't possess it. His motivational refrains helped improve my negative thinking when it was cratering. The persistence with which he surrounded me with love and friendship changed my operational definition of friendship; it redefined relationship for me. It also sparked a lifelong commitment to ministering to other men to foster the same growth and change I experienced.

Ironically, Ty later disclosed that there was a reciprocity in our friendship that I didn't see at the time. He communicated years later that the way in which I pursued my wife inspired him to be a better husband. He said he never saw, before or since, a man who loved his wife as much as I loved mine or worked as hard to win her heart back. He also shared that he was moved by my persistence and willingness to not tap out. That many times since, when he had a bad day, wanted to give up in the face of adversity, or simply was in a bad headspace, he thought of me, in the worst of my days, and it helped him to persevere.

Ty also knew me before, during, and after the marital issues G and I had, and he told me he's never met anyone who has changed as profoundly as I have. I was able to reprioritize my life in ways that made him reconsider his choices. I pivoted away from the acquisition of wealth and toward balance in ways that helped him create a different hierarchy of needs for himself and his family. I often thought of my relationship with Ty as one-sided, in that he poured into me when I needed him the most. That is largely true. But what I ignored is that when a man is persevering through struggles, he can still be a light onto others and an example based on the way he carries himself through the shadows. Even the weak can sharpen the strong and help remind them of how to be closer to the man they seek to become.

Sharpening others

I mentioned above a commitment to lifelong ministry that came out of the support Ty showed me. Our relationship completely flipped the notion of male friendship on its head for me. He gave me encouragement. He provided support. He demanded I do more than I thought myself capable. In many ways, he carried me before I could walk. I knew the value that held for me at the time. I also knew I wanted to offer that for someone else. I'd done it for years as a therapist and a coach. But this was different.

I wanted to help another man become better because someone had done it for me. My only payment? The knowledge that I could share my experiences dealing with difficulty, as well as the gratification of supporting someone else in dealing with their own difficulties. This process of discovery, support, camaraderie, and friendship that was only afforded through another man's accountability would be an amazing gift for someone else, just as it had been for me. I just needed the opportunity.

And as the universe so often does, it delivered precisely what I was seeking.

The Case of Derrick

DERRICK AND I had been acquaintances for years. He reached out to me, saying he and his wife were having trouble in their marriage. He knew Gina and I had been through it, and he wanted to sit down and share some of what they were going through to get some tips, advice, and perspective.

Derrick and I got deep into it, and fast. Truth was, we didn't have a choice because when he called me, he was already in a state of crisis. He was transparent about their marriage troubles. His wife said she was unhappy in their relationship, felt disconnected from him, and was frustrated by his acting out. The word divorce had already come out of her mouth. She had one foot out the door.

Derrick was willing to try anything to fix it, but he needed some sharpening, for sure. My first step in doing so was to impress upon him his role in the current situation and encourage him to take accountability. Before we sat down, Derrick was doing a lot of blame shifting and buck-passing to his wife. He said their sex life was down and out, complicated by their having five kids and him working and traveling so much. He mentioned that he struggled with porn, but by default, because his wife wouldn't avail herself to him. Derrick was unhappy at his job and had been overlooked a few times for promotions he felt he deserved. He felt undervalued, mostly by his wife. He didn't feel like she was doing her part to support him, help him, and love him well.

My sharpening of Derrick started the same way Ty's sharpening of me did: getting next to me in my mess. We spent a lot of time together, getting to know each other deeply and sharing space with each other, which allowed him to drop his guard a bit and trust me as his friend and sherpa through our collective journey to hell and back. If the sharpening was going to work, he needed to feel comfortable enough to let me into his mess and open himself to what I had to share with him.

But unlike Ty, who approached my situation with empathy and endless compassion in the form of his presence, I needed to shift gears with Derrick. The work required immense shifting of Derrick's approach. Sure, mine with Gina did too, but Ty's role was to be my cheerleader and lift my spirits. I needed Derrick to dig in and change his ways if he wanted to have any chance of success. Sharpening, for Derrick, was more about punching him in the teeth, metaphorically, and less about being a warm blanket for a hurting friend.

First thing I did was spotlight the corrosive nature of his porn use and how it was obliterating the intimacy with his wife. I forced (not asked) him to admit that with five kids, his own crazy work schedule, and being at home with kids crawling all over her all day, it would be impossible for his wife to find him desirable upon entry into his home every day. Her ability to find herself ready, willing, and able for sex had, by that time, been virtually all but eliminated based upon his persistent use of porn, which (by the way) she had caught him engaging in on multiple occasions. He came into his relationship with me with the belief that he was using porn as a remedy for their lack of intimacy, which was solely her choice. Truth was, he was solving on her behalf, not seeing her perspective, and pushing her farther away from him, and in an area in which she wasn't lobbying for a solution. Derrick selfishly took matters into his own hands, furthering the effects by implying that his wife wasn't enough in the process. My sharpening of Derrick helped him see that his choices and his lack of availability drove her away, and it was now his responsibility to draw her back in.

Derrick was also stressed beyond belief at work when we first started our conversations. He didn't feel respected; he experienced his role as being cast aside and passed over, and he was losing motivation. As a result, he came home stressed and took it out on his kids and his wife. He experienced difficulty managing his mood and making decisions. Those issues needed to fix themselves quickly as well if there was even a modicum of hope for a favorable pathway ahead for the couple.

Sharpening Derrick in these areas led to an insistence on making different choices, both at work and at home. In this area, and in all areas of our discussion, I was transparent about the changes I made to win Gina's heart. I cut back at work dramatically. I willingly participated in individual therapy to help me change my disposition and implement those changes to focus on what mattered: my wife and my kids. Derrick heard this loud and clear and began to make those shifts as well.

What grew out of that work with Derrick, now almost five years later, is one of the strongest relationships I have on Earth. Derrick started by gradually opening up to me about all of his mess—their issues, their communication, their intimacy, his vices, her frustration with him, and how close they actually were to calling it quits. In the beginning, when things were at their worst, we were doing whatever was required to manage the crisis, much like how Ty and I operated in the moments when G and I were at our worst. But later, our sharpening was guided by my own sharing of my personal issues and challenges, how I responded to them, and ways in which Derrick could use a similar approach to restore balance in his family and rekindle his marriage.

I'm pleased to report that although those things aren't perfect, they are much, much better for Derrick and his wife. They are still married, and they have much healthier communication and a much more active sex life. Derrick has almost completely eliminated pornography from his daily activities, and in the instances where he slips up, he is honest and takes accountability. He doesn't travel anymore and works a much more manageable forty-five hour week, which has produced favorable results in terms of how he is received by his colleagues. He was recently promoted to a high-level leadership role in the company, with a big pay bump and a team at his disposal. Now, he feels respected and much more confident because he is seen by others for the value he can bring to the table. Derrick feels like he has command of his life. His relationship is bearing the fruit of his effort and renewed energy.

We need each other

Twenty years of practice as a mental health professional, thirteen years as a father, seventeen years as a husband, and one near-failed marriage, which we've rehabilitated into something very special, have taught me one main lesson about being a man: To actualize our potential as men, we require the presence, friendship, and accountability that only other men can provide through deeply connected, honest, and trusted relationships. Men need to be sharpened, and only one man can sharpen another, as iron sharpens iron.

Despite anyone's best efforts to be fully autonomous and independent beings, in no way reliant on anyone else, men need the company and friendship of other men. Men need the deep connection that comes with being around one another. It helps us maintain balance in our existence. It reinforces positive behavioral choices and steers us away from acting out. Men also benefit from the feedback, guidance, and direction that only comes from the advice and redirection a friend and brother can provide. Men are wired for independence, which sparks loneliness, which leads to acting out. Positive male relationships help diminish these unproductive predispositions.

Men struggle with being open and vulnerable. As a result of our closed posture in our communication, we have difficulty talking about our feelings, our fears, and even our goals and desires. To better hone these tendencies and build beneficial skills, men need practice. Male relationship helps us practice our communication with one another. Friendship gives otherwise closed men the opportunity to share their thoughts and emotions safely with greater transparency. To become better communicators, men need to practice sharing. It doesn't come naturally and takes risk and the willingness to fail in order to truly grow as a man who can communicate his experiences in a genuine and honest way.

Becoming honest

The sharpening of other men allows us to become honest with ourselves. Often, as men, our insecurities and defensiveness erect walls that disable us from hearing the feedback that inevitably helps get to the truth. As men, we puff up, misrepresent, avoid, or sometimes downright lie. We are fearful of judgment. Fearful that people will see us as less than. Fearful that other men, to a certain extent, will laugh at us, mess with us, or embarrass us if we share the deepest parts of ourselves. Being transparent about who we are, what we think, and what we want and need makes us feel exposed. Yet in feeling exposed, we become acquainted with the reality of our situation.

When I shared my burdens with Ty, he responded with love, care, and support in precisely the right measure. It was instrumental in my getting well from a mental health perspective and a necessary ingredient in my desire to keep going. His sharpening of me, albeit gentle in nature, revealed my truth: I was unwell and in an extremely dark place. That was hard to admit—particularly to him but also to myself. But in that admission of weakness and vulnerability came my true and earnest understanding of the scope of my problems. As he and I shared more about my challenges and my relational issues with Gina, my sharpening included the necessary steps in pursuit of fixing those issues and accountability to ensure those things were happening on a daily and weekly basis without regression or exception. In fact, it was my honest assessment, made possible only through the mirror that relationship with another man provided, that helped me take the right steps and in the right sequence. Those steps led to a successful reconciliation of our marriage, which was on life support at the time.

A byproduct of my struggles with Gina and the relationship Ty and I forged is how many relationships of substance I've built with male friends since. I take great pride in that. I've helped many of those guys in various ways. Derrick represents a shining example of that willingness to pay it forward and use my experience to walk alongside another man struggling in a similar fashion.

One of the most beautiful things about being a man is that many men share similar experiences and wrestle with common themes: the burden of leadership; work/life balance; the demands of being a husband or a partner in a romantic relationship; being a son; being a friend; and determining what is most important in life based on all the roles we inhabit. Given the prevalence of our common experiences, and the hardwired messages we receive from the world about the benefits of self-reliance, men often sort through these experiences in isolation, thereby limiting the process of essential learning that relationship affords. The truth is, when we do so, we are robbing ourselves and one another of the benefit of doing things side by side in relationship.

I was able to help Derrick because I had weathered the storm in the fight of my life to save my marriage. I fumbled through improving as a communicator. I struggled through radical transparency with my wife, particularly when it was hard. I rearranged my life and my priorities to be around so I could effectively build and rebuild relationships. I made hard changes. But what made the difference for Derrick was that I led with fear and vulnerability. I opened myself and modeled how that looked and felt. I stood next to him in his own garbage. But I also flipped my own pail over and sorted through all the trash right in front of him. Ty provided a space for me to do this. I shared what I learned about myself with another man to help him move through his mess.

Sharpening can be firm and abrasive. And it can be soft and persistent. But both sharpening and being sharpened are required for men to be good men.

TIPS FOR GUYS

Relationships take time, effort, and patience—especially with other men. Don't get discouraged; meaningful connection is a lifelong process. Stay committed and play the long game.

Give other men grace. Building relationships is hard for many of us. Men aren't naturally wired for deep connection—it takes learning, patience, and practice.

Men need accountability from other men. Honest friendships help us see ourselves clearly, make better decisions, and follow through. Real growth comes through the mirror of relationship with other guys.

TIPS FOR PARENTS

To help someone grow, you need to be present. Carve out time and space in your busy life to invest in others. True sharpening requires space and availability.

Sharpening others is taught by example. If you want your kids to value service, they need to see you modeling it. Your actions set the tone for your home and for the young men you raise in it.

Dads, don't fear other men investing in your son. Exposure to wise, quality men strengthens him. It doesn't replace you and doesn't have to threaten you—it expands his growth, character, and vision.

LESSON 7

Gentle Strength

What is strength as a father?

THE PRESENCE of a male father figure is one of the most essential ingredients in the successful growth and development of a family system. In the absence of effective male leadership, individual families, and our society as a whole, start to break down. The data tells this story very clearly. According to nolongerfatherless.org, 85 percent of youths in prison come from fatherless homes. Seventy-one percent of high school dropouts come from homes without a present dad. Ninety percent of all homeless and runaway children hail from single-parent households. And in the most staggering and most unfortunate statistic of all, 60 percent of youth suicides occur in homes where no father figure is present. If you question whether a strong father in a healthy home is essential, these facts show just how much of an impact a father makes on the entire system.

But it's not just about a father's participation in the family. They need to lead their families too. Men need to be strong for their families. Men need to make hard decisions. They need to support their wives and children. They need to protect. They need to serve. They need to keep peace. They need to speak up in challenging situations.

Yes, families need strong men. Women have a need for strong husbands. Sons and daughters need a strong presence to cover their household so they can feel safe. When children feel safe, they feel supported. They work harder to seek the affirmation of their parental figures, and they are willing to take healthy age-appropriate risks, confident in their father's (and mother's, but certainly father's) position to receive and embrace them should they fail. A strong father is instrumental in the development of healthy children, as wives feel supported, encouraged, and safe in the presence of a confident and solid spouse.

Sons also need strong fathers as role models of what strength looks like—what it means to work hard, what it means to be humble, what it means to be self-assured but not cocky, kind but not soft, firm but not overly aggressive. Young men and men all learn, first and foremost, what it is to be a man from their fathers through modeling at a very young age. Strong fathers set the right kind of precedent as their boys begin their progression through manhood.

So, what if you're not strong enough?

Sometimes dads aren't strong enough with their boys. Dads often desire to appease their son and make him comfortable. They prioritize their son's own comfort over safety or what is in his best interests. This value judgment probably comes from a good place: Parents want their boys to feel safe, supported, and comfortable in their journey through life. But when these examples are either persistent or severe in their nature, this becomes a critical and grave mistake that people make.

It is not your job to be your son's pal; it is absolutely your job to do whatever is required to keep him safe and alive. It is not your job to prioritize his comfort. It is your job to hold him accountable for his behavior. All of this must be guided by relationship and responsible decision-making. I will always take an aggressive stance to stop parents from shielding their son from discomfort because of their own anxiety or fears about his potentially negative response.

Parents often lower the bar for their son by not demanding his best. They allow their sons to do things that are easy instead of hard, murky instead of morally upright, or risky instead of conservative and appropriate. These situations typically stem from prioritizing our son's happiness over his best interest. Far more times than I can count, I've seen parents look the other way on issues like underage drinking, watching suggestive content, and getting a cell phone or social media too young to ensure their son is comfortable and content. Unfortunately, in doing so, parents send a message that he does not deserve their best efforts, and worse, they don't care if he is actively doing something irresponsible that can cause him harm or expose him to danger that could have dire consequences.

Parents, specifically fathers, have an obligation and a primary responsibility to act on behalf of their son's safety, encouraging responsible decision-making and engaging in conduct of integrity, irrespective of social choices. Oftentimes, those situations require an aggressive and swift response of discipline. Fathers who fail in these instances hate to see their kids unhappy, listen to them incessantly complain, or live in a world where other people are doing something that their son isn't. These are hard choices and even more difficult to sustain over time, particularly as kids age, mature, and seek more autonomy. But being too passive or gentle as a father can have direct consequences. This is why strength, conviction, and clarity are needed from Dad. Absent that, Dad, you're often exposing your son to something he should not be doing. Thus, you need to immediately shift gears and make a different decision.

One example of the need for strength as a father is in situations related to safety. When safety is at risk, it's essential to get your message across so it is effectively received by any means necessary. Sometimes a little dose of shock and awe is effective in underscoring the scope and severity of the situation. The truth is, when your kid is in danger, how he receives that message of safety is of absolutely no consequence. It is the job of the father to get his point across in these situations, no matter what. The art of yelling as a father is a skilled discipline to master. And it's a fundamental ingredient in effectively sharpening your son.

But when is strong too strong?

It's important to have a father who is strong in his convictions, his presence, his commitment to the family, and his general demeanor and tonality. Typically, strength and power are associated with aggression, physicality, stature, and gravitas. All of these elements, in the correct measure and enacted with consistency, can make for effective fathering. But what happens when these attributes are present in excess? When is strong too strong?

In my twenty years in mental health, I've far too often been around dads who have swung the pendulum of masculine energy way too far, resulting in counterproductive effects to the rest of the family. In some cases, Dad's success, influence, charm, and charisma have led him out of his home and into the arms of a younger, bubblier, less demanding alternative, often leaving an eviscerated family in his wake. Sometimes Dad's fundamental and innate desire to provide a quality of life for his family that he can be proud of makes him feel overworked, highly stressed, and underappreciated at home. In those instances, Dad shows up as snippy at best, abusive at worst. When Dad's spirited demeanor morphs into a hot temper with limited margin and lack of freedom of flexibility, this can manifest as verbal or physical abuse. Strength is necessary for dads, but it's not strength in isolation we're aiming for. It's gentle strength.

The easiest way to define gentle strength is to examine some clear examples of how I've seen it manifest in a clear and solid progression. I'll also take the liberty of mapping two cases that can serve as helpful examples to provide a basis of comparison. In one, Dad was far too gentle. In the other, Dad was far too strong and abrasive, causing significant harm to his kids. The hope is that through an examination of these three different scenarios, we can understand the ideal balance of gentle strength.

I felt like my strength made it hard for me to understand

Some of the same issues impacting my relationship with G made it more difficult to connect with my daughter, Giovanna, especially when she was younger. I was often too busy at work and didn't make time. I failed to adopt a curious posture, lacking in my ability to ask questions and seek to know her, and instead I made assumptions about what she needed or wanted. I lost my cool more times than I care to admit and was abrasive or aggressive in my tone and delivery when it wasn't warranted. Too busy, too important, too guarded to make myself vulnerable and seek to know. Some of the very same traits that make me strong led to me fostering a weak connection with my own daughter years ago.

As a result, Giovanna seemed to be closer to my father-in-law, her uncles, and even my own father. The distance between me and my daughter became more prevalent once G and I started having issues in our marriage and when I started doing personal work in therapy to take self-inventory and examine my own struggles. I'm fairly certain the distance was mainly due to Giovanna simply spending more time around these other men than she did with me. I worked too much, carried myself like I was working too much, complained about working too much, and treated those around me like I was working too much. In my absence, other people stepped in to fill that void.

But it wasn't just a lack of proximity that was hurting our relationship. It was my demeanor: wound too tight, too stressed, too aggressive, too quick to anger, and too ready, willing, and able to use profanity (which I remain to this day, despite near Herculean efforts to curb this). My rough exterior made it hard for me to connect with my daughter on her level. In most of the ways we assess and evaluate masculine strength—aggression, emotion, work ethic, proclivity to take initiative—barriers impeded my ability to be gentle and welcoming with my own baby girl.

I was also running on empty. Emotionally, I was fighting for my marriage with everything I had. At that time, work was challenging in the volume of hours logged and the emotional toll of the job. It was also dangerous; I was doing crisis work 24/7/365 that was life threatening in nature and immature in its infrastructure at that point in the business, given that we didn't have a well-developed team or processes that allowed me to delegate work. As a result, I didn't have the energy to invest in my relationship with Giovanna. Underneath all of that was what usually lies beneath: fear. I was afraid that I couldn't connect with her if I tried. An exterior of strength concealed my fear about my own prospective ability to be an effective father to my daughter.

I'm embarrassed to admit I thought those things some time ago. But the truth was, my desire for self-preservation, my fear of trying and being rejected, and my lack of emotional bandwidth made it easier for me to opt out during the first two years of her life. Even more embarrassingly, I felt as long as I made enough money to employ a full-time nanny who basically raised our kids alongside my mother-in-law while they were young, then I was doing my job. Back then, I measured my contribution to my own children in units of billable hours and take-home pay.

But most of all, I was a one-dimensional version of myself. I didn't understand or prioritize relationships effectively. I wasn't balanced in terms of my time or my interests. I didn't have enough margin or mind space to consistently carry myself well, irrespective of circumstance. As such, I was driven, aggressive, and influential. But I lacked leadership, humility, and gentle strength.

Being too strong and in no way gentle made me ill-equipped to love and adore a woman of any age well.

Healing myself

Only in healing myself could I lead with a gentle heart in reimagining the relationships with the most important women in my life, specifically my wife and my daughter.

In *Fathered by God,* John Eldredge discusses the phases of men's lives and the corresponding behavior that characterizes each phase. According to Eldredge, "At nearly every stage of our masculine journey, something in us needs to be dismantled, and something needs to be healed" (213). At the Boyhood level, the child seeks the affirmation of his father to reinforce a sense of value and self-worth from within. I had issues with the security of my attachment based upon the challenges of my own relationship with my dad. The insecurities that welled up in me as a result of my parents' divorce and my father's coming out impacted all of my substantive relationships thereafter. As a result, deep personal work was required for me, particularly as I had to purge myself of my anger and learn how to develop a gentle demeanor alongside a strong persona.

How to be more gentle with others

I wish I could trace back to my turning point to share with all the dads how the change came about in me and in my relationship with Giovanna as a result. The transformation took place over years, through lazy afternoons playing dress-up as detectives who were hunting for clues in the woods and singing in the car to the *Frozen* soundtrack on repeat. It was at snack time when I cut the crust off her bread and at bedtime when she refused to go to sleep, despite my best efforts. It was in the sum total of the smallest and seemingly most incidental of moments when I really got to know my daughter.

I will, however, point to some of the principles I came to live by when parenting Giovanna that I hope all dads will consider when working to build a better relationship with their children—their daughters in particular. These concepts can help sharpen dads so they can be more gentle with others, especially those who matter most.

1. Be available

The first step to parenting effectively and making connections with your kids is simply being there. This requires time and the willingness to connect. In the first half of my marriage—the first eight years until things between G and me completely blew up—I was busy working, and when I wasn't working, my mind was occupied with work. Thus, it was difficult for me to be physically present or emotionally available. Adjusting my priorities and making more time to be available felt uncomfortable at first. It was hard for me to fill the space with my kids one-on-one, particularly when I was working to spend that time in meaningful and impactful ways after a previous deficit.

Now I recognize there is value in just being there. Sitting next to her and watching a show. Driving her to and from dance and listening to Taylor Swift. Helping her straighten her room when she's stressed and overwhelmed. Delivering her favorite snack—a bowl of Lucky Charms—when she's spending quiet time in her room. Now that I'm around more, it's more comfortable to spend time in ways that do not require as much energy. When I wasn't spending as much time with the kids, I felt pressure to squeeze every ounce of juice out of the time I was alongside them. Being available has meant less pressured time, more enjoyable exchanges, a more relaxed posture on my part, and a greater flexibility and dynamic for both of us.

2. Establish and uphold a consistently safe posture

As you've probably gathered, being gentle doesn't always come naturally to me. But in therapy, I learned the degree to which my anger, volume, and emotionally volatile existence permeated the household. Mess in the physical space would make me anxious and easily frustrated. My work life was so chaotic that it helped my mind if our home was clean and tidy. Having company often caused me to come undone as

I was so fatigued from fourteen- and sixteen-hour days that I would lash out or snap at G and the kids if people were at the house when I got home. I was never abusive—just loud, grumpy, and quick to anger, which made my wife and children feel like they needed to walk on eggshells (even before my kids knew what eggshells were).

I had to accept that truth before I could take steps to address it and improve upon it. Little girls don't need to be screamed at by their fathers. It doesn't work, it isn't effective, and it sets a horrifically negative precedent for the future of the relationships they will share with the men in their lives. For me, abiding by this principle meant I stopped yelling whenever my daughter was present. If G and I were arguing, I would immediately stop whenever Giovanna would walk into the room. If I wanted things to be different, I had to transform my tonality, delivery, and aggression in the home, at least in front of her, for starters. This was not easy but was an essential component of my daughter and my wife both being willing to see me as someone who was safe and inviting for them to be around.

3. Enter her world

Next, I had to take off my old worldview and, in every interaction with her, enter into hers. Little girls want to be beautiful, they want to dream, they want adventure, and they need to feel pursued, especially by their fathers. I had to seek my daughter's heart if I wanted her to let me into it. This meant adopting a curious posture and experiencing the parts of her life that brought her joy.

A few years ago, this meant things like taking her and our

new puppy, Chicken, our adorable little Cavapoo (who still sleeps in Giovanna's bed most nights), to dog-friendly Home Depot and pushing them around in the cart together, or taking her to the beach with me so she could pick out the perfect spot to build sand castles. Now, it's lattes at Starbucks, a $10 limit at Target so she can pick the best knickknacks she can find, or driving around listening to Taylor Swift. It took a genuine investment of my time to understand who she is as a person and embrace doing what she enjoys.

4. Seek to know her heart

It's one thing to know her interests and enter into her world; it's entirely different to have your ten-year-old baby girl trust you with her emotions. It means I have needed to demonstrate a consistent tone, delivery, and communication style, with any deviation from that pattern demanding that I take steps to repair it.

It also means being immensely patient with her emotions, especially when they might not make sense. For example, because she's young and highly emotional, many of her behaviors aren't super mature or rational. Sometimes in the morning, she'll completely lose it when her hair doesn't come out the right way or when she can't find something to wear. She needs the right water bottle, not one of the ones that her brothers use, and nothing else will quite do. It's in those moments when I sometimes find an upwelling of frustration that I must work against to avoid yelling, disciplining, or making threats. That type of response is hard for her, and she completely shuts down in the face of it, regardless of how grounded the approach is. As a result, I must seek to understand why she is frustrated, emotional, sad, lonely, or angry at her siblings. It is my responsibility to ask questions in an effort to help her get to the right answer. I try to reinforce that I am seeking to know her and better understand what she is going through so I can help her in whatever way she needs.

The Case of Edwin

MANY BOYS' acting-out tendencies function as grand gestures of seeking attention, most specifically from their identified father figure. They want to see whether their father and other older men will embrace them unconditionally. I've worked in situations where, because of their jobs, busy travel schedules, and positions of influence that require time and attention, hyper-successful dads are often largely absent. These busy dads are disproportionately hands-off with their sons, functioning as far more passive than the moms who are running the show without them. In these cases, I've seen dire consequences for sons who innately seek the strong presence of their father. In the case of Edwin, my intervention provided the direction and clarity he was sorely lacking due to the passivity of his father.

Edwin was skinny, wore glasses, and had acne. He didn't show up with a lot of social confidence or clout. He was short, too, probably under five feet tall and not even one hundred pounds as an eighth grader. He wore modest clothes that also reflected his own self-appraisal. His parents had outlined for us a significant history of bullying, which explained why Edwin kept poor eye contact, didn't have a firm or confident handshake, didn't have many friends, and typically just stayed in his room and played video games. But it didn't explain why he was explosive with his mother. He would frequently blow up at her, talk about how much he hated her, and share his frustrations and overall general mindset that she was the worst person on Earth. She certainly wasn't. But she made him want to explode.

Unfortunately, Dad and his son had no relationship whatsoever. He attempted to hold the kid accountable, particularly when he spoke to his mother in a disrespectful manner, but it never worked. There was no foundation of respect and connection there; those are necessary ingredients for effective discipline and accountability to occur. As a result, his parents let Edwin get away with basically everything. Mom's strategy was to use the family's abundant resources and buy him new things in order to appease him. Go-carts, PlayStations, Xboxes, mopeds, paintball guns, pinball machines, air hockey tables. You name it, the kid had it, which is why his world was always under assault. They attempted to incorporate consequences by removing those things, but in truth Edwin had nothing he sincerely valued, including the possessions that were given to manipulate and gain his affection to achieve a brief armistice. Edwin had no positive prosocial relationships. He was not enrolled in any activities after school. All he wanted to do was play video games and get lost in the abyss to escape his daily life.

Bullying

I didn't really understand the extent to which the bullying occurred. We only found out about it while making the decision to send him to treatment. He kept a journal hidden from his parents in a hole in the wall behind a poster in the closet. It was not intended for anyone to ever find. Mom, in fact, put her hand through the poster accidentally while cleaning out his things to prepare for his departure for treatment, revealing a secret storage compartment filled with hidden treasures and secrets. In the notebook, Edwin had outlined the horror he faced:

"You should just go kill yourself!"

"You're the biggest loser that has ever lived."

"Your mom probably wishes you were never born."

"You're a mistake."

"This is why you have no friends."

Edwin heard these kinds of statements on a daily basis. Some of this was being done via cyberbullying, and this was one of the first cases twelve or thirteen years ago in which I navigated instances of young men being victimized in that fashion.

Hurt people hurt people. It was clear where the rage Edwin aimed at his mother had found its origins. Once I read the journal's content and put it up against the parents' report about his mood and extreme anger, I concluded that Edwin was in danger and needed to be sent away immediately. Mom and Dad wanted to take a wait-and-see approach. I felt we needed a greater sense of urgency and a more immediate plan. I put a framework in motion to move toward a higher level of care to give Edwin the help he desperately needed.

Mom agreed and realized that the circumstances were not going to improve with traditional once-per-week talk therapy alone. They needed something bigger and more comprehensive to address the circumstances more swiftly and aggressively. Treatment was supposed to be that avenue.

I could tell in Dad's body language that he was waffling when he first sat down with me for the intervention consultation. Yes, he understood intellectually what I was saying, but he wasn't convinced it was the right answer. Nonetheless, he acquiesced. He said he understood all of the steps and went along with Mom and me at every turn during the planning process. He provided his credit card for the nonrefundable payment, willingly communicated with the transport folks who would escort his son, paid the retainer to the placement consultant who would select the precise option for Edwin's needs, and even booked the airline tickets.

But something in my gut made me feel less than satisfied with the situation and less than secure in my own position to manage the circumstances. I just wish I'd been able to diagnose it sooner.

I thought I could reach him

I got a phone call very early on the morning of the day of the intervention. It was Mom, screaming and crying. All I could make out was that she couldn't find Edwin anywhere. He had left a note saying he'd spoken to his father. He had run away from home and wasn't coming back.

The note said Dad had told him what was happening. He blew up our plan.

I immediately called the father and told him to be in my

office at 8 a.m. He told me he had a patient who he was scheduled to prep for surgery at 7:30 a.m.; I told him to cancel and that I would plan on seeing him at 8 a.m. He begrudgingly consented and met me in the lobby. There was no one else present in the office at the time. That was a good thing.

He sat down, and I could tell he was nervous. Turns out, Dad felt it was important to tell his son the details of the upcoming intervention. He felt, in his words, that "he could reach his son," and it was important for him "to share the news directly so that Edwin wouldn't be taken aback by the information, scared when he arrived at the intervention, or surprised in any way."

It's relevant here to highlight what an intervention is and why it's important to do one well. An intervention is a planned conversation that provides an identified individual with the feedback that their life is unmanageable because of their substance use and mental health issues and that an immediate change is being mandated by their loved ones as a result of their choices. If you've ever seen the show that bears the name, an intervention functions much like it does on TV. Parents have prepared often-emotional statements conveying their reasons for concern. There is a designated order for who speaks and when, based upon the relationships and the degree of influence those individuals have. An ultimatum is provided that offers support immediately but outlines the consequences if the individual refuses the support being offered that day.

Most importantly, under no circumstances can the client have advance notice of what might happen. Individuals can run away, harm themselves, or worse if they know they are being forced to leave their family to go to treatment. Because the stakes are so high, the situation must be handled in the right fashion by a trained professional. Orchestrating the intervention precisely and according to plan highly increases the likelihood that the client will take the help being offered to them. Unfortunately, I've seen interventions mishandled on many occasions throughout my career because individuals shared key details or did not adhere to the well-defined script.

When I found out Dad tipped his kid off, to say that I was irate is one of the great understatements of my professional career. I make no apologies for how I handled the situation. It was necessary to convey my response deliberately, outlining the gravity (and now danger) of the situation.

A guy walks into an operating room ...

"I understand that you are a surgeon?" I asked him.

"Yeah, yeah, I am," he responded, eager to share the details of his esteemed career. "I've worked at the hospital a very long time. You know, it's been great. I've been able to help a lot of people and save many lives. It's a career that I feel really good about being able to carry out as my life's work."

"That's awesome," I quickly responded, still not yet beginning to reel in the catch I had just snared, happily trolling the line instead. "I think it's great that you've been able to help people in such a way for so long. You know, I'd imagine it took a tremendous amount of training to be able to be prepared for those types of high pressure, critically urgent situations."

"It did. It's something I take a lot of pride in and try to not take for granted."

"Cool," I said. At this point, I was anything but. "And so,

let me ask you a question: When you walk into the operating room, is there a specific procedure that you have to undertake prior to surgery?"

"Of course there is," he said flippantly. "We have to lay out all of the instrumentation—the nurses mostly do that, make sure the tools and the operating room itself are sanitized, hook the monitors up before the patient even comes in, and then when the patient comes in, there's a million things you have to do to get them prepared, depending upon what type of specific procedure it is."

"I mean, yeah, that makes sense. I'm sure it takes a lot of time to get the scene ready and to plan and prepare in advance, to get everything ready to go," I said. "I only have one more question for you, I think, before we get started. How would you feel, after all the work that's required to plan in advance and make things safe, and in spite of the years and tens of thousands of hours of training, education, and practical experience you possess, if I ran into your operating room, grabbed a scalpel, and started hacking up your patient? How would you feel then, given all you'd done to help them get well?"

An unsurprising silence washed over the lobby where we stood staring at each other, our hands in our pockets. He obviously didn't know what to say.

"What would you do if I overextended in your ER? Worse yet, what could be the consequences if you allowed me to do so on your watch? The same as the consequences might be if we can't find your boy. Grave."

And he just hung his head.

Dad's desire to be his kid's pal superseded the abilities and acumen of the only guy in the mix who possessed the training and the experience required to oversee the situation in a safe and correct fashion. When people overstep and try to do too much, they introduce an element of risk that has no place in circumstances like this.

Lowering the bar

For a guy who ultimately wanted to help his kid, it was a sad realization that he had actually done something to harm him and put him in danger. The good news is that Edwin came back. I eventually convinced him to sit back down for the actual intervention so we could safely send him off to treatment. Granted, I had to misrepresent the situation to do so, but I was able to come to peace with my deception relatively easily; he was far safer under our watchful eyes and with accountability from the team than he was when he ran away. After all, he was actively having thoughts of harming himself and was on the run from his folks.

Dad had good intentions. He didn't want his kid to be uncomfortable. He was concerned, based upon his son's bullying history, his mood, and his anxiety, that he would be shaken and upset by the element of surprise that came with the intervention. He was worried his boy would hold it against him. Worried his son would dislike him or that the separation and space between them would only continue to grow based upon a hard decision to step in and send him off.

For me, these are easy choices. Safety wins, always, in instances like this. A child's preferences remain a distant second to what must be done to preserve a young man's health and wellness and move him forward in his life, particularly when he is struggling. In this situation, a dad must be strong enough to understand what is right for his family to make a difficult decision, especially when his son finds it unpleasant or worse.

The Case of Shawn

I'VE SPOKEN PERSONALLY about how my overly strong demeanor and sometimes harsh behaviors caused harm to my nuclear family. This observation required my attention and energy to make the kind of personal improvements that would eventually lead to effective changes on the home front. As a strong dad, I let my work get in the way, I was primarily focused upon myself and my own goals, and I was hyper-regimented and hyper-disciplined to the extent that Gina and the kids paid the price. These tendencies were deeply rooted and took years to untangle.

Here's one more example (albeit even more extreme) of how a strong dad can be too hard on his son. How the desire to hold a young man accountable can spin out of control and render irreparable harm. How a father's words, intended to sharpen and call his son to action, left a young man bruised and even scarred.

Shawn was a "Causeway of Old" type, one of the rougher kids we've had through the center. He came to us at sixteen when an in-school fistfight rendered him suspended for ten days. The other kid involved said some things about Shawn's mother that he, for good reason, didn't like. Shawn's response was to force him to leave two teeth at the scene of the crime courtesy of a right cross that would have left a competent fighter down and out. Shawn played both hockey and rugby at a high level. He was a tough kid by any and all metrics. A true guy's guy.

But, ironically, alongside that, Shawn was one of those "good kid" types, too. He went to church with his family every Sunday. He wore a cross around his neck, the one his grandmother gave him for confirmation before she passed. He said hello to all the elderly men and women as he walked in and out of church, and any of them who knew him well or had a granddaughter around that same age would say, "Ya know, we should introduce Shawn to [insert name of wholesome American girl the same age]." Most parents would be more than comfortable with Shawn being in the presence of their daughter.

Shawn had a great relationship with his mom, too. They would grab a slice every Tuesday after she picked him up from rugby practice. They watched episodes of *American Idol* together every week, debating who would win as the contest came down to the wire. They started getting really tight after Dad took a big promotion that brought him to the West Coast for work. As a result, he scooped up a swanky townhouse in Bel Air and commuted into LA every Sunday through Thursday for work at one of the largest PR firms in Hollywood. It was an opportunity too good to pass up, but for this dad, it wouldn't have mattered. Shawn's dad didn't say no to anything in the work domain. Under the guise of "providing a life for his family that he never had," he wanted to make sure his wife could stay home. It was important to him that the family had a membership to the private country club in town, not the public one. Shawn's dad was completely self-made, and he made sure as many people as possible knew it. He worked harder than most people ever should, which is how he found his way to a C-suite at a PR juggernaut.

As a result, Shawn was the man of the house. He stepped in to try to parent his three younger sisters. He studied hard and got good grades, determined to find his path to a school on scholarship. He drove himself to practice, drove himself to the gym, and made sure to put in two to three hours per night on his studies. Shawn was pushing hard to achieve his goals but was burning the candle at both ends.

It's unsurprising, then, that he broke when his father's tough side got the best of him. Shawn had stayed out late after the hockey game, a game they won 3-2 when he had an assist on the final play. He had far too many beers and came home pretty drunk. Definitely an error in judgment by Shawn and absolutely something he deserved to be held accountable for. But he certainly didn't deserve what he got from Dad that night.

He was verbally berated and traumatized by his father to a degree he would never forget. His father's words and actions left a permanent imprint on who Shawn became. Upon coming home drunk, Dad told his son "he was a piece of trash," that he "wished he was never born," that he was a "mistake" and an "embarrassment to his family's good name."

From there, Shawn responded brashly. "If all those things are true, then maybe I should just go ahead and kill myself," he told his father. As he wiped the tears from his eyes, he immediately regretted his words. But for Dad, tough as nails, old school, and quick to fly off the handle, he simply wouldn't accept those words coming out of his son's mouth.

He would make an example out of his son. He would belittle and embarrass him.

The shouting match occurred on the front lawn. In Shawn's recollection, his father said, "I'll be right back." He stomped toward the front door, swung it open, and came back out with the biggest knife Shawn had ever seen. Dad then flipped the knife at Shawn's feet on the grass. Shawn was both shocked and confused.

"Do it," his father commanded. "Do it, you fucking pussy. If my one and only son wants to be a pussy and leave his parents without a son, then you might as well. Go ahead, you coward."

When Shawn rehashed what his father said that night (granted, it was hazy given how drunk he was at the time), those were the heinous words he recalled his father saying in disappointment and rage. It broke Shawn.

Years later

Ironically, Shawn is doing great. He still remembers that night—it's burned into his memory. Since his drinking was the catalyst for the incident with his father, he's never had another drink. He went to a top college, got an academic scholarship, and has since graduated and works at a huge consulting firm for six figures right out of school. By some metrics, Dad's aggressively strong approach to his son seems to have worked.

But Dad made a decision that was wrong for one primary reason: It introduced risk. He verbally challenged and verbally abused a minor under the influence of substances, encouraging him to take his own life and directly providing him the means to do so. This leaves far too much to chance, particularly with the understanding of just how impulsive young men are, especially when provoked. Dad's strong approach shifted abruptly into being reckless and irresponsible when he encouraged the unthinkable for his only son.

But even more than this offense being irresponsibly unsafe, Shawn's dad permanently changed his son's sense of self. Saying your son is trash and a mistake and you wish he was never born are words that can never be taken back. These traumas frame how we think about ourselves forever as men and imprint themselves on our hearts. They inform how we see ourselves, how we develop relationships with others, and how we live our lives. Traumas like the one Shawn suffered become a part of who we are and seep deeply into the fabric of our DNA. What was meant to help a young man become a better version of himself immediately devastated his ego, broke his confidence, and shifted his experience of becoming a man in the world.

Finding the balance

In responding to the shifts in my posture toward and conduct around my daughter, and in examination of their own treatment separately, my sons give me a lot of grief and aggravation. They joke that whenever they do anything wrong, they get held to the stiffest of accounts. In contrast, they feel like I speak to Giovanna by saying things like, "It's okay, Boo-Boo Bear … don't you even worry your pretty little self about it." When Giovanna wants help or a favor, I'll gently respond to her and say, "Of course I'll get you cereal and bring it to you in bed, my lady." This led to a bold declaration by my boys: I treat the two of them in a completely different fashion than I treat their sister.

Most parents would lie, deflect, redirect, or shirk responsibility in answering to this claim. Instead, I leaned into it with all I had.

"You're damn sure right, boys," I responded. "My job as Giovanna's father is to guard her heart and keep her safe. That requires that I am soft and gentle with her. And love her a little bit differently. But sons, my job with both of you is to sharpen you, to mold you both, to hold you accountable, so you can both be the most extraordinary men of God that you possibly can. Although I hope we get along, I actually know that when you're pissed at me or when I'm frustrating you, I'm doing my job well. So if you want me to be gentle and soft on you, just say so. But if you want to be extraordinary, then I'll keep doing exactly what I have been."

Neither one of them offered a syllable in response. I guess you can be sharpening one kid while being gentle with another, even under the same roof.

Later that week, my daughter got into a fight with her brothers at dinner. Giovanna told her brothers that she knows she's Daddy's favorite because we go on dates all the time and do fun things, and I always take her side and stand up for her, and I never yell at her like I do both of them.

Ironically, the boys actually shared her perspective but for completely different reasons: They each felt they were my favorite—mostly because we spend so much time together and thoroughly enjoy the same things.

For me, this was a significant achievement as a father and one of the few I have been able to hold as a positive barometer of my own self-worth. My kids believing that they are each my favorite is a sign that my efforts to convey love and affection to them are working. It's also an indication that I've found a good balance between gentle and strong. Being strong allows fathers to hold their children accountable, police their kids' behavior, create high standards, and make children more motivated to work to achieve their potential.

But a father's strength can never overshadow a gentle quality of support: kind words that can help a young person feel comfortable in situations of difficulty. Emotional availability for a child who is suffering through pain or hardship. A calm, consistent demeanor that perseveres in the midst of familial unsteadiness. A peace that settles and relaxes an otherwise anxious home.

Gentle strength is our North Star as fathers. And though I'm nowhere near where I need to be, I appreciate the steps I've taken to learn a new and better approach as a dad and the progress I've made along the way.

TIPS FOR GUYS

Balancing strength with gentleness takes time and practice. Becoming a strong man isn't about perfection—it's about growing through trial, reflection, and connection.

Being gentle isn't weak. True gentleness is strength under control—choosing kindness, compassion, and grace even when you have power. It's a consistently calm and measured presence, not passivity.

Women need the safety that gentle strength creates. Consistency, empathy, and emotional control build trust and connection in relationships.

TIPS FOR PARENTS

A father's presence is critical—but strength must be balanced. Harshness undermines leadership. Aim for gentle strength: firm, compassionate, and steady.

One outburst can undo months of calm. When we slip, it's essential to own it quickly and apologize well. Accountability restores trust and models growth.

Be present. Time builds trust. Simply showing up—again and again—creates safety, comfort, and space for your loved ones to be fully themselves.

LESSON 8

Find Your Thing

Win or go home

IT'S THE FOURTH QUARTER. It's win or go home. We've had mostly a down season, as is to be expected for a young and inexperienced team. In a combined league of sixth, seventh, and eighth graders, we've got a quarterback who's a sixth grader (my oldest son) as well as a determined fifth grader who starts at corner (he happens to belong to me as well). We've also got a head coach in the form of yours truly who has a tendency to wear his emotions on his sleeve, particularly in games that come down to the wire, like this one.

We're waging war in the SFFL—the Shelton Flag Football League. It's a modified 8 vs. 8, full pads flag football league, using live wrap-and-pull rules, without tackling. In an era when football is declining in popularity at the youth level because of increasing concussion awareness, it's a desirable alternative to tackle football. For a dad who loves football but who is also trying to be responsible and sensible on behalf of his boys, this was a no-brainer for us as a family, especially when my boys were young.

Game on

We're limping into this elimination game as the 3-5 Vikings, who have underachieved by every metric of evaluation. We're squaring off against the 4-4 Chiefs. But we're in this one, and if we can find a way to win it, we'll play our way into the tournament against the top seed. At that point, all we have to do is win. There's a minute and a half left, and we're driving. Game on.

My eldest son Vince takes the ball in the shotgun. Vincey's the QB1 for us, standing five-foot nothin' and a mean eighty-seven pounds. But he's tough and persistent, and he protects the football well. He's outperformed expectations for a sixth grade starting quarterback.

We've been down all day, but a touchdown at the start of the fourth quarter cut the lead to two. At that moment, Vince rolls to his left, evades the blitz, and extends the play before the rush catches up to him. Right before he gets pushed out of bounds, he pulls up and launches the ball downfield toward his favorite receiver, who is somehow wide open in the back corner of the end zone. Touchdown. We go up 26-22 with fifty-three seconds left.

The place goes nuts—pure pandemonium, at least as far as middle school football crowds go. I've been a dad for more than twelve years now, and this was easily a top five moment of my dad career, no doubt. My son, who grew up with a football in his crib, who started out skinny, undersized, uncoordinated, and not much of a football player, just chucked a dime to win the game and send us to the playoffs.

All the while, his brother, who is ten and weighs seventy-one pounds, held it down for us all year at corner against bigger, older players. He, by virtue of his effort and drive, proved to himself and his teammates not only that he belongs, but that he is as good as anybody we have in the secondary. I felt an overwhelming sense of pride for both of my boys and gratitude that they were able to experience such an iconic moment of preteen triumph.

The unthinkable

But then, as can happen occasionally in sports, what seems impossible actually comes to pass. The opposing quarterback, coincidentally leading the Chiefs, gave his best Patrick Mahomes impersonation and started driving his team downfield as time ticked off the clock. QB draw for twelve yards with the clock stopping as the chains moved. Tight-end drag across the middle of the field for seventeen yards as their coach rushed to call time out. Then, the impossible occurred: The quarterback dropped back, evaded the rush, and hit his wide receiver in the back of the end zone on a post corner as time expired. Chiefs 28, Vikings 26. Game over. The very same group of triumphant preteens who had started posing and gesturing to the stands forty seconds earlier had their hearts ripped right out of their chests.

As soon as we shook hands, the entire team collapsed onto the ground, faces down, in tears. Over their audible sobbing, I asked these boys to gather in a circle and looked every single one of them in the eyes. Fighting for their respective breaths, they listened with blank stares, tears in their eyes, and mucus dripping out of their noses.

"Boys ... in football and in life, sometimes things go your way. And sometimes things don't. Tonight they didn't. And just like life, when they don't, it sucks. And it's hard. And you get emotional. And you're angry. But I'm here to tell you all something: Right now, despite how you feel, you are a better young man and a better football player because of what happened to you just now. It doesn't feel like it, but it's true. And I'm going to tell you something else: If you come back here, and if you want to be a part of it, you're going to get another chance next year to make this right. I'm hoping you'll take it alongside my sons and me." With that, we wiped away the tears, packed our gear, and walked off the field with our heads held high.

For years, I'd made excuses. I'm too busy. It's a long season. I'm responsible for too much at work. I even convinced myself it would be better for someone else to coach my boys because it would be too much pressure for them or it would adversely affect our relationship. Year after year, fellow coaches and other dads had told me I should coach, but I perpetually made excuses about why I had too much on my plate to take on the commitment.

Coaching youth football for five seconds helped me realize that none of that was true. Coaching youth football was very obviously my thing.

Finding a thing

Since the inception of Causeway, a single unifying principle has guided my work with men and young men: the belief that every person has "a thing." Their thing. A unique desire to pursue a single interest with everything they have. A thing they can immerse themselves in for hours on end, tirelessly pouring themselves into it without it feeling like work. They often already possess an aptitude for their thing, and once they find the drive to do it, their thing evolves into something more than just a proficiency—it becomes a purpose. In sum, everyone has a calling that pulls at their soul. Our mission, as young men and men, is to set out on the business of finding that thing and pursuing it with all we have.

In guiding young men for nearly two decades of my life, my intention has been to walk alongside them and help them find their thing. This can be a difficult process. The truth is, finding one's thing can only happen through trial and error, iteration, feedback, redirection, and a stick-to-itiveness that allows one to keep going. Where does one start? Truth is, it doesn't matter. It just matters that a young man begins to gain experience, learning at every phase of the process about his likes, dislikes, skills, gifts, and motivations.

Finding that thing is no small endeavor. In working with three thousand young men and their families, I've seen more people fail to find their thing than succeed. One reason is that passion isn't always able to be reconciled with commonly held sensibility. Worldly parameters—the desire to make money, one's employability on the open market, and having a role that fits comfortably within a family lifestyle—shrink the frame of the given choices at our disposal as we seek to find our thing in life. Sometimes, prioritizing the conventional—like time at school, time to do our homework, and time to hang and spend time with friends—pushes up against the freedom and flexibility that allows us to aggressively pursue our main thing. In this day and age, particularly for young people, time is in short supply.

Most people don't ever really get to find their main thing. However, in seeking one's thing, the guiding questions are actually relatively simple and straightforward. I believe zeroing in on a young person's main thing begins with this question: What is the thing that person would do for free for as much time as they could and with the greatest degree of enjoyment, forever? Finding something that doesn't feel like work and turning it into a job is the best directive I could give any young person.

It is essential for a young man to work tirelessly to find his thing because the boost that occurs when he wraps himself around something he is passionate about is unlike any force in the universe. A young man needs a quest, a goal, a mission—a destination to dream about, to work toward, and to chase. In order for that thing to be effective in making him a better version of himself, it is utterly irrelevant what that thing is. It simply doesn't matter. It just matters that a thing exists to orient the life of a young man and ensure that every other thing in his life falls under the umbrella of pursuing that goal.

Think of a funnel. It's wide at the top, narrow at the bottom. This is how we approach finding a thing. We pour a bunch of stuff in when a boy is young—sports, music, chess, theater, academics, working with their hands, etc. Some of it sticks; some of it falls by the wayside. But as we move through life, we filter out the inputs that don't represent our thing and get closer to a more refined version of what our thing actually is. Three sports become two sports; two sports become one. Sports plus music becomes either-or because the demands of doing both are unsustainable. Eventually, our thing requires so much effort and work that we can pursue no more than one, maybe two if we are efficient with our time and willing to push ourselves with our effort. As we move forward, we refine our pursuits, getting closer to what that thing actually is.

The people around us assist us in clarifying what our thing is. In developing relationships with others who share similar traits and similar gifts, our peer groups will drive us toward our calling as well. We keep the company of those like us. Those whose tendencies we gravitate toward will serve as mirrors of the direction we are heading. As we learn and grow, we become more like them. We develop deep-rooted relationships with people who share the same passions. What we value in them, admire about them, and enjoy about sharing time with them helps young men understand the qualities in themselves that they seek to accentuate as they move forward in life. The company we keep represents who we want to become and helps us better understand who we are.

In helping our sons find their thing, we need to give them room to explore. We need to be okay with their exposure to things we don't understand. Many parents, for example, don't believe their son's thing is in fact a thing. I've seen many guys come through our doors in the last decade who believe being an influencer, a DJ, or a professional video game player is, in fact, their thing. Most often, that's smoke, distracting their parents from their sons' true intention (to be left alone) and giving them more room and space to mess around online. However, those things are in fact things as well. When pursued with passion and purpose, they can be lucrative, complex, and highly technical, and they certainly can become careers. We need to do our best as parents to afford our sons the flexibility to try new things even if we don't believe they are real and even if we don't find value in them ourselves.

Why else is a "thing" important?

The consequences for a man who doesn't find a thing can be dire. When a man can pair his work with his gift or his calling, life is difficult, but it requires far less energy and difficulty each day. When a man works within his calling, he is more motivated, able to be a more effective leader, possesses more capacity and bandwidth outside of work, and feels more rejuvenated by his work on a daily basis. He is more driven to excel and put forth his best. He can stay planted, and he typically experiences less movement over the course of his career. Men can also develop better relationships with people both inside and outside of work when their job and their passion represent the same thing.

Does your work have to be your thing? Not necessarily. Many men have jobs, and they have their thing in addition. For some, the qualifications associated with their thing don't allow them to do it at a professional level. I've had clients who love skiing, bowling, gaming, music, bodybuilding, hunting, fishing, and all sorts of sports, but they weren't quite good enough to do those things to make a living.

But this is where our Wild comes in. We need to nourish the parts of ourselves that fuel our soul. Many guys have a skill *and* a thing. The thing—the gift, the calling, the passion—is what we do as men that doesn't feel like work. And that can be our work, but it can also be our thing. Regardless of the category, we need to hold onto it tightly and continue to do it all our lives.

Having a thing creates a sense of order in the life of a young man. It allows boys and young men to make decisions more readily, to rank and file their choices, and to determine what they want to sacrifice, how, and in what measure. Having a thing helps motivate them to work harder, to work longer, and to sustain their attention in a world where every day, our attention is a bit more fleeting.

Why is it becoming more difficult for boys to find their thing? Today, more than ever, it's harder for boys to figure out precisely what that thing even is. Young people are more distracted as technology consumes more of their time than ever before. Young people are also distracted in more precise ways by uniquely curated inputs that consume their attention in a surgically invasive fashion. The algorithms young men bump up against in their daily lives become smarter with each collision, persistently providing the precise stimuli that will render them helpless against a daily onslaught of pinging, purchasing, streaming, and chatting. All of us—young and old—are flooded: Our time is flooded with competing demands, our schedules are bursting with to-dos and must-dos, and our minds are overflowing with noise. In the midst of that incessant avalanche of inputs, it's difficult to make anything a main thing.

As discussed in Lesson 5, young men also quit a lot. Unfortunately, this occurs far more than it used to. If we're quitting more frequently and faster than we used to, it's harder to immerse ourselves in something for a long enough period of time that we can grow competency in a chosen path. To have a thing, you can't just say you have a thing; you have to pursue it wholeheartedly for thousands of hours to grow in both passion for it and competency in it. Malcom Gladwell tells us that it takes roughly ten thousand hours of deliberate practice to become world-class in a given field. Today, it's tough to get through the first couple hundred hours before we either quit something, get distracted, or decide to move on to something else.

This chapter highlights how I came to find my thing outside of work, which helped me become a well-rounded version of myself and establish more balance in my life. I'm fortunate that my work—helping young men become better versions of themselves and navigate life's transitions—is also my thing, since I was a young man who lost my way. But as I got older and intentionally reduced the emphasis of work in my life to prioritize my family, I found my *other* thing.

It also highlights how Henry found his—how he walked the path from a depressed shell of himself to a young man making his way in the world with a clearly defined passion and thing that lifted him out of his pain and defines the life he lives now.

The opportunity

After holding out for years to coach football for my boys, I begrudgingly started out as an assistant, helping Coach Rob by serving as his defensive coordinator when my boys were eight and nine. Ironically, when I look back now, I'm nostalgic for those days, with all of the benefits and none of the extras. No emails. No parent correspondence. No scheduling issues.

No questions. Just show up, teach the boys how to cover, fire each other up, and, if time permits, where to actually line up. Perfect. We weren't any good, but it didn't matter. I realized I needed to coach my sons and coach football in general. Being an assistant coach was light work, so it coincided with my degree of willingness at the time. But it didn't take long for the pilot light to ignite. Watching my own boys get better. Teaching the kids something new and having it work. Helping them do more than they believed themselves capable of. I began to want more.

Then, as it always does when you get an itch about something, the opportunity manifested. Rob and his son were moving over to play tackle football, leaving the junior varsity head coaching role open. It seemed to be a perfect fit, so I called up the commissioner of the league and introduced myself. I told him I'd supported Rob the season before and wanted to take on the open spot, and both my boys would be on the team. The commissioner responded with trepidation.

Apparently, the varsity head coach was also stepping down, leaving a vacancy at the top of the organization. Typically, the commissioner explained, whoever was selected as the new varsity coach would bring in his own personnel. "So," the commissioner advised, "if you want to coach your kids, the only way to guarantee you can do that is to take over the varsity job."

Made sense. I just didn't like the answer. Same old excuses. I'm too busy. It's a long season. I'm responsible for too much at work. It's better for someone else to coach my boys because it would be too much pressure for them or would adversely affect our relationship. I only wanted to coach the junior varsity, and the truth was, I didn't want to be a head coach; I only wanted to help. I definitely didn't want to be responsible for two teams, as I only had my boys on one. Honestly, it felt like a lot of thankless work.

I told G about the situation. I shared with her what the commissioner said, conveyed to her my excuses, and waited for her to let me off the hook. But she knows me in her bones and knows what's best for me when I can't yet understand it for myself.

"Let me ask you this … you want some hack coaching both of your boys for the next four years while you sit back and watch, wishing it was you?"

I accepted the head coaching positions of the Shelton Vikings, both junior varsity and varsity, later that night.

My own stamp

Coaching has given me so much more than playing ever could. I love the kids—each of them in different ways. Coaching gives me the opportunity to learn about each of them: what motivates them, what's their capacity, what do they want, how do I help them achieve it. I love to motivate them in ways that are catered to their individual personalities, to get more from them than they believe they can muster, to push them beyond the scope of what they might have thought possible on their own. I love seeing things that other coaches don't, scheming by identifying a small detail, exposing it, and building a game plan around it. I love the parents. Not the interactions with the parents—the emails, texts, questions that I can't answer—but the faces of the parents watching their son accomplish something they didn't think he could, or even better, that he didn't think he could. I love bringing people together. Most of all, I love the sum total that results when the kids start working together to become a team.

As a man, coaching has been a wonderful outlet to develop new relationships with men I've never met, to put my unique stamp on a group and bring guys together who, without football, would never cross paths. We've put together an amazing group of men who give their time, all their effort, and significant resources to help these kids be better football players and better humans in the process. Prior to coaching, I didn't have these kinds of friends. Now, I have brought together a group of guys who are all close and whose sons have strong relationships with each other as well.

Coaching has also helped me be more social, meet new people, and spread goodwill, and it has served as a meaningful conversation starter across contexts. I've given a lot to be a football coach, but it has paid back in spades in elevating the depth and quality of my social experience with the friends I've made and people I've met for the first time. I'm grateful that G called me out, knew what pitch to throw, and that I was willing to listen and act on her advice.

As a father of sons, it has always been essential to instill discipline in my boys. As a result, I've done my own fair share of yelling, correcting, redirecting, and encouraging. I've put a premium on squaring them up, adding my two cents in an effort to ensure sound judgment when appropriate, reinforce their strong character, and affirm consistency on their behalf. But those are definitely not the best parts of being a dad to my boys.

I've learned, in fact, that the best part of being a dad isn't molding them into strong young men of character, although it is something I take great pride in. My favorite part of being a father to my sons is standing alongside them as they do what they love. But for us—Vince, Leo, and me—it's not multiple things. For us, it's one thing, our thing: football. And on this canvas, I am both father and coach, and they are a meld of my sons and my players. The memories we have forged in this landscape are unlike any that we've experienced together.

The Case of Henry

LIKE MY OWN KIDS, Henry was fortunate enough to have found his own thing. Like my kids, Henry's parents sought to know their son and support him. And like my kids, Henry's thing helped him step into becoming a version of himself he felt proud of.

For much of his life, Henry faced challenges across a great many domains of functioning. He struggled with symptoms of both anxiety and depression. His executive functioning skills had always been poor. He was popular among his peers, but sensory issues created struggles around physically feeling comfortable in his own skin, even if he conveyed a demeanor of comfort externally. He struggled with body image, and his weight had always been a problem, both as a child and a young adult.

Henry came from an affluent Jewish family from the city. Dad was a Yale educated lawyer who was an executive for one of the big sports franchises that we all know and love (or love to hate, depending upon what side of the fence you're on).

Mom met Dad at Yale, where she also got a law degree, and she had a bustling career in finance, in addition to managing and overseeing everything for her three children for the entirety of their lives. This was, by the operational definition, a powerhouse couple; however, they were entirely different from any other family I had worked with.

They were overwhelmingly patient with their son and saw him for who he was. They took stock of his issues and empathized with his personal struggles. They afforded him latitude, accepting parts of him that were difficult, such as his marijuana use, because it provided an inroad to redevelop and solidify their relationship, particularly as he transitioned back from his mental health treatment far from home. Mom and Dad supported Henry unconditionally, never pressuring him to be someone he was not. These tendencies differed dramatically from many of the "upper one percent" couples I had worked with in the past, who typically exchanged kindness, acceptance, and patience for accountability, persistence, pressure, and deliverables. These folks were absolutely brilliant and accomplished but also kind to their boy, seeing him and loving him for precisely who he was.

How Henry got to treatment

They decided to send him away to treatment during his junior year of high school because, well, there just weren't any other options. They hoped if he went away the summer before his senior year, he would get himself together and then perform well enough in school to apply at a great college.

Henry's treatment was absolutely necessary at that juncture. It started with a complicated medical situation.

In a freak twist of fate, he fell off his skateboard (with his helmet on) but hit his head on a rail at just the right angle while attempting a new trick. He fell at just the right angle and suffered a severe concussion even while wearing protection. Henry, whose health had been impeccable prior, as he was a decorated soccer and squash player, competing at the highest levels in both sports, started suffering from debilitating migraines, dizziness, lethargy, and other symptoms he couldn't shake. His concussion was labeled severe by all of the neurologists his parents consulted. All came up empty in their desire to effectively treat his symptoms.

On top of that, Henry started running with a rougher crowd. He was no longer able to play sports because of his head trauma and the lingering consequences. The only thing he ever said was helpful in remedying his symptoms was marijuana. Desperate for peer acceptance and a community where he could feel connected, Henry sought the comfort and friendship of guys who liked to smoke weed. His friends' personalities and vibes fit well alongside his easygoing, casual, laid-back disposition. His parents recognized this, which is why they approached the situation with such leniency. Despite functioning as a star athlete in his life prior to his accident, Henry never really was able to connect with the aggressive, rah-rah, douchey jock types. The stoner guys were more his speed. Eventually, given the connection with new kids and the respite from his consistent headaches, Henry was smoking weed three to four times per day. By the second semester of junior year, he was high virtually 24-7.

Henry's life ground to a screeching halt in terms of his daily functioning. He stopped going to school completely, smoked marijuana constantly, and was extremely depressed. His parents became fearful that his wellbeing was rapidly declining. He stopped eating, bathing, brushing his teeth, communicating with his friends, and even leaving the house. There were no signs he was a danger to himself or someone else, but he simply wasn't experiencing any joy nor was he able to accomplish the most basic of tasks. He was growing physically weaker every day, having lost nearly fifteen pounds on an already rail-thin 5-foot-11, 120-pound frame. It was a scary situation for everyone involved.

Henry was never an oppositional kid, so when his parents and a mentor sat with him and explained the benefits of going to treatment, he understood the upside and agreed it could be productive. He acknowledged it could be the kind of space where he could have a hard reset, clear his head, and get better. The trouble was, he just hadn't prepared for what lay ahead.

It broke him

The treatment program broke him. It was far and away the most traumatic experience of his life. On many occasions, his parents had given him assurances that if there were any issues, he could hoist the white flag for help and they would send assistance, no questions asked. At a moment's notice, they would extract him from the program, bring him home, reevaluate the situation, and start again. By day two, he was crawling out of his skin and shouting from the mountaintops, "Get me the fuck outta here!"

Henry couldn't deal with the seemingly endless restrictions and BS rules. His diet was already challenging to manage, and the vegan/vegetarian diet for program participants didn't agree with him due to preexisting sensory issues and personal taste. It was hard for him to eat at all as those problems quickly worsened. By the third or fourth day, he was completely shut down, fully isolated, borderline nonverbal, extremely depressed, and having thoughts of ending his life. He plotted an escape plan: He would cut a hole through the fence, burrow his way through, and take his own life before being apprehended and brought back to camp. Thankfully for all parties involved, the staff upped his supervision so he was unable to do so.

As much as it broke him as a young man, Henry's time in wilderness therapy eviscerated his relationship with his parents even further. Wilderness therapy, broadly, is a modality of residential treatment that is set in a remote location. The premise is that rather than having care be rendered in a sterile, clinical, hospital setting, the lessons and approach function as a metaphor for overcoming obstacles that are applicable to the world at large and are set in the wilderness itself. In theory, a wilderness program possesses utility. However, these settings have been highly controversial over the past few years as many celebrities have been outspoken about their allegedly inhumane or abusive experiences while in wilderness therapy.

Prior to his time there, his connection with his parents was exceptional. His send-off and stay created a canyon of space between him and his parents that he had never thought possible. Prior to departing for therapy, he only felt their unconditional love and good vibes in their exchanges. Afterward, he hated them, didn't trust them, was often unwilling to even speak to them, and didn't engage with them for years because of the trauma he endured. He felt completely betrayed, cast aside, left behind, and othered. It was a difficult and dark time for him—and for his parents by extension.

Other layers

Henry was a brilliant kid but never put the effort into school because he felt that no matter what he did, he could never hold a candle to his genius Ivy League brother, a fellow squash player who got a full scholarship to Princeton, or his far more productive little sister, who was a star—equally smart, even more compliant, and a resident family genius in her own right. He was stuck in the middle and always felt like a piece of garbage, seeing himself only as a burnout who could never quite put forth his best.

There was another layer here, too. I hypothesized that even more than his inferiority complex related to his siblings, Henry never felt like he could get out of the massive shadow cast by his Ivy League-educated parents. The truth was that as I grew to know all of them, I saw that he was just as smart as any of them. In fact, Dad would say he was smarter. This kid was a whiz with people, lightning-quick on his feet, with a magnetic personality that made him a joy to be around. Everyone who knew him—friends, family, teachers, therapists, people in town, coaches—loved him. He had a nice way about him and a pleasant disposition that made him easy to like, no matter what kind of person you were. Henry, unfortunately, hated himself and didn't have a sense of confidence, which made it difficult for him to feel good about anything he did or the plans he was making for his life.

Their relationship

Henry and I worked together for many years after he left wilderness therapy. For the first year and a half, our primary objective was the rekindling of the relationship and the reinstallation of trust with his parents. Their kindness, patience, and love for him never wavered. But it was important for them to demonstrate to him on a daily basis that they accepted him unconditionally, no matter what he did.

Given the state of their relationship and the need for them to come back together and heal, I was far more lenient than usual in advising this family around issues such as his illicit drug use and his purchasing of drug paraphernalia. I felt it was essential for him to build trust back with his folks, and vice versa, for him to be accepted in spite of his challenges, and for them to demonstrate to him that their love was unconditional.

In Henry's eyes, implicitly, his parents had communicated that their love was inherently conditional, based upon their unwillingness to bring him back home immediately when he arrived at wilderness therapy and conveyed his initial dissatisfaction with being there. According to Henry, his instincts were screaming loudly that this wasn't the place for him. His parents listened to the urging of the staff, which was to hold the line and let the treatment team do the work of engagement with Henry in the milieu. But Henry felt deeply rejected despite the fact that this was clearly not the message his parents intended for him to receive. And so we worked, week after week, session after session, just so his parents could show him their relationship was solid, they were a present force in his life, and they loved him no matter what.

The saving grace

Through all of his difficulties and pain, the saving grace in Henry's life was music. In music, Henry found his thing. He was a decent drummer in high school but had never received training. But the mentor whom I mentioned previously (the one who sat him down and discussed program placement) was highly skilled in coaching kids on the college selection and application process. She identified a narrative for him that tied his time at wilderness therapy to drumming, his music, and a deep personal awakening. Henry put in the work and turned that vision into a masterpiece. His college essay was pure gold.

He ended up getting into Berklee College of Music in Boston, one of the top five musical conservatories in the country, not only because of the coaching on the writing of the piece but quite frankly because his aptitude was incredible. The kid picked up drumsticks late in the game, and without much technical training, he was very good compared to the average drummer—certainly good enough to get into a college music program. This upside catapulted him to a place where he could compete amongst the upper crust of musicians. It was important for him to demonstrate that on a regular basis, and although he lacked the confidence to do so when he got to college, he was motivated to put in the work and perform at a consistent level. He worked hard every day, improving in his process and his approach as he went. It was a slow but steady progression.

Henry shared with me that during the first couple of classes, he felt like a joke and a fraud. He thought he was less than everyone else and didn't belong, particularly in the presence of highly technical musicians who had been aggressively pursuing their crafts for their entire young adult lives. But he kept showing up, and he kept working at it, and he kept trying to get better, trying to learn, grow, and improve. That's what people do when they really love something: They pour themselves into it until they get where they want to be, and they never quit. Henry never did.

The life source

Henry is now a senior in college—it's his fifth year, actually. His parents have supported him the entire way; they saw value in his giving himself extra time so his pathway was more manageable and comfortable. Because of the family's love for their son, unconditional patience, and surplus of resources, they never wavered in their commitment to him. I still talk weekly with his parents and with him as we consistently modify the strategy for what he needs. Yes, he has many challenges—he lacks focus, he's not committed to his daily wellness, he doesn't take care of himself, he suffers from chronic pain, the trauma is still there, and other reasons make it hard for Henry to be his best version of himself on a daily basis.

But through it all, music has been the constant, the through line, the life source. The drumsticks and the drum pads have kept him afloat. Music gives him a vision for his life post-college. Absent that, there would be absolutely no motivation, or no vision, for that matter. He doesn't know if he wants to be a performance drummer, an agent, or a music teacher. I don't think it really matters; he's the kind of guy who's going to feel happy wherever he goes as long as music is involved. As long as his parents continue to demonstrate their consistent love and patience for him, I'm confident he will get where he wants to go.

I'll also bet that place will be extraordinary, no matter where he ends up.

Magic

In the noise of busyness comes the peace that stems directly from being consumed by a thing. In sports, it's sometimes described as "being in the zone." This flow state represents what happens when time slows down, the world around us makes sense, and we see things almost in slow motion as they happen in front of us. This elevated state of being comes from the unique pairing of passion and aptitude.

When the person doing a thing boasts a hunger for that endeavor, and nothing stands in the way of that objective, the result is magical. This optimal approach occurs, for the greatest, alongside otherworldly performance that can only be built through tens of thousands of hours of intense work and preparation behind the scenes. Tom Brady down 28-3 against the Falcons. Michael Jordan in Game 6. Taylor Swift on stage in front of more than eighty-five thousand fans, dancing in the pouring rain to a standing ovation. In some situations in life, a person is exactly where he or she should be, doing precisely what God created him or her to do, showcasing their talent to the world.

Our thing

The night of the Chiefs game, when Vincey threw the almost–game winner, he collapsed into my arms in the driveway when we got home, sobbing. He couldn't speak. As I held my son, crying so hard he couldn't catch his breath, I didn't speak either. I just rubbed my hands through his hair for a while. After he had cried himself out, I looked him in the eyes and told him, "You did everything you could. You gave it all you had. You're going to get your turn. I promise."

As a football coach for three seasons, I've won a bunch. I've also lost a bunch. I've seen my own boys fail and succeed in their own rights. But honestly, it's being alongside them and having such an overwhelming amount of time with them, doing something we all love, that's been the most meaningful. It's the windshield time we share to and from practice, where we game plan, talk about personnel and who's good on the other team, and where we can focus our strategy. It's talking over dinner in January about who's coming back next year, when the season doesn't start until August. It's being around their buddies, hosting them in our home, having pool parties for the team to develop camaraderie before the season starts. It's taking them to buy new spikes and gloves and visors, and all other forms of drip.

The truth is, the things I love most about football now have nothing to do with the score. It's fathering my sons in an entirely different way. It's using football as a metaphor to teach them about life. To believe in themselves. To believe in one another. To set a goal and hold themselves accountable to it.

Football isn't really about football. It's about learning to apply lessons learned inside the lines to everything beyond the gridiron.

But honestly, what I love most about football is that it isn't my thing; it's our thing. Leo, Vince, and I. In finding their thing—without my prompting, or pushing, or negotiating—we made memories together that we will always share.

TIPS FOR GUYS

Finding your thing is essential in becoming the very best version of yourself. A young man needs a quest, a goal, a mission—a destination to dream about, to work toward, and to chase. Having a thing creates a sense of order in a young man's life. No matter the challenges in pursuit of one's thing, the essentiality of a central force in a young man's life cannot be ignored.

Resist the temptations that present as barriers to finding a thing. Young people are more distracted than they have ever been. It's hard to sift through and fine-tune choices, paring it down to just one point of focus. Surgical focus is worth it because the payoff that comes with finding a thing can function as the guiding principle in a young man's life.

Zeroing in on a young person's main thing begins with this central question: What is the thing you would do for free for as much time as you could and with the greatest degree of enjoyment, forever? Finding something that doesn't feel like work and turning that thing into a job is the best directive I could give any young person.

TIPS FOR PARENTS

Help your son find his passion like it's a team sport. He needs your support through time, resources, guidance, and encouragement. Be present, show up for the milestones, and actively back his journey. Your involvement helps turn his interests into real growth.

Never discourage your son from pursuing his passion—so long as it's safe, legal, and growth-oriented. What the "thing" is doesn't matter. What matters is that he has one. Your role is to support, not steer.

Never force your passion onto your kid. My sons and I share a love for football—but it was their choice, not mine. I gave them options, supported their interests, and only stepped in as coach with their permission. What they choose matters less than the fact that they choose. Help, but don't direct.

CONCLUSION

What happens when you get there?

WHAT DO YOU DO when you actually arrive at your destination? How do you feel when you have accomplished the goal that once felt impossible? What do you do when you spend months or even years working the fields, sowing seeds, planting and watering, and praying for rain? When you pray, wait, pray more, and wait more, out of necessity? And one day, the rain that you have been so eagerly and desperately waiting for finally comes. What do you do then?

At age forty-three, I had arrived at a place where I was living a more abundant life than I ever expected and was more content than I ever imagined. These blessings were not measured in dollars or billable hours. I was living out the future that I could have never envisioned some thirteen years ago when I embarked upon this insane Causeway journey.

My wife and I found ourselves happier than we had ever

been, thanks to a small fortune spent on therapy and a great deal of personal work, commitment, and grit. My kids were healthy, happy, engrossed in solid peer groups, and able to pour themselves into pursuits they loved. They each had a thing. For Giovanna, it was dance. For Leo and Vince, it was football. We live in a nice home, have wonderful friends, and surround ourselves with positive people. Our work matters, too.

One text message

But at any point, at any second in our lives, we are but one text message away from our world being shattered. My text message came on July 7, 2025. It read:

"V- meet me at Yale. The Dr. said I have to bring Leo to the emergency room right away."

From there, our journey into the unspeakable began.

It's been three months of horror—for Leo, for his mother and me, for his siblings, for everyone who knows him. Turns out that he has an incredibly rare blood disease—Severe Aplastic Anemia—that impacts about two out of every million people in the United States and Europe. Essentially, Leo's bone marrow is failing, which means that he is not producing enough healthy blood cells. He requires a bone marrow transplant to have the opportunity to return to living a normal life. Absent that transplant, he would not recover.

In fact, I'm writing this conclusion from his room on the Hematology/Oncology wing of the seventh floor of Yale-New Haven Hospital. He's three days into chemotherapy that is intended to completely eradicate his old and defunct immune system, which will be replaced by new cells via transplant in the coming days. By a miraculous occurrence, my son was paired with the only 10/10 non-sibling donor match who existed for him in the worldwide bone marrow donor database. We may never meet that individual, but he or she has agreed to be a donor in an effort to save my son's life.

Right now

Ironically, just when I thought I had developed and understood these eight lessons enough to attempt to share them with the world, I'm finding myself relearning and reapplying them in entirely novel ways. Right now, we're building a new life as a family, **Brick by Brick**, given Leo's diagnosis. It means different things for all of us—Leo not attending school, restricting our social lives, prioritizing circumstances differently, working remotely to limit exposure to germs and potential illness. But we have a clear blueprint for the road ahead; one that, if we adhere to the guidelines as suggested, comes with a 90 percent or greater success rate for our son. We are in the early stages of gut-renovation of our life, but we collectively find comfort in the plan and ground ourselves in a present-centered, brick-by-brick approach to taking it one day at a time. Frankly, any more than one day at a time would be too much.

As his father, I've had to **Name It to Tame It** with my own fear. I've had to admit to my sick son that I am afraid of the road ahead, but that I trust God's plan for his life, and trust that this trial will be used for good. I've communicated to his brother and sister that being brave is doing a hard thing while admitting to yourself that you are afraid as you march forward. Acknowledging that something is hard, but persevering through it, is the way to manage and tame our fear as men.

I've had to resist every fiber of my being, which told me to pour myself into my work to get through this season. I've reminded myself that **Provision Is Not a Substitute for Presence** and that being alongside my son during his trial carries a value deeper than anything provision could ever offer. It would be easier for me to default to my workaholic tendencies, to busy myself with tasks, and occupy my mind. Instead, my wife and I have shared this time with him, side by side, for every second this summer, and counting. We've attended every transfusion—Monday, Wednesday, and Friday—for as many as eight hours each day for eleven weeks. Now we're inpatient at the hospital for another six weeks until his transplant is complete and he is fully recovered. There are many other places I could be at this moment; sitting beside my son's bedside is the only one that matters, because presence reminds those around you that they're not in their fight alone.

I've been humbled throughout this experience. As a man who has devoted much of my adult life to **Finding My Inner Wild,** I'm learning that wildness doesn't always look like mountain peaks, adventure, or freedom without limits. Sometimes, finding your Wild means laying it down temporarily. In this season, I've traded nature, freedom, pleasure, and extravagances for hospital rooms, medical clinics, and working entirely remotely in a part-time capacity from a laptop. I've surrendered pieces of what feel most like me—but only for a time, and only for the sake of something greater. I've shrunk my world so that my son's world might one day expand beyond measure. And I'm realizing that sometimes the hardest, most courageous Wild is in the fight you take on for the people you love, even when it looks like nothing you've ever known.

Leo has personally reminded me that, no matter how bad things look, it's your job to **Never Tap Out.** But the truth is, this superhuman effort is a consistent and collective push from the people he loves most. When he first learned about his diagnosis and that everything in his life that he loved—football, lacrosse, basketball, fishing, and riding his dirt bike—would be taken from him until further notice, he certainly wanted to quit, but he refused to tap out. When the doctor told him that he would be out of school for the entirety of the school year, he fell to the ground sobbing and screaming. It was I, as his father, who stepped in to lift him up—physically and metaphorically—when he didn't want to keep going. When he was told about his impending bone marrow transplant, and the fact that he would receive chemo and radiation and be an inpatient for a minimum of six weeks, his mother's love blanketed him, calmed him, and softened the blow. Sometimes, not tapping out is being resourceful and relying on the people in our boat to help row forward in the face of our own trials.

One of the hardest things I've faced in all of this has been the limiting of our social relationships. I've learned in the last decade or so that **Iron Sharpens Iron: Men Require Relationship** with other men. I'm at my best when I have other guys in my life on a weekly basis. These relationships give me both healthy accountability and encouragement. Discussing common struggles provides a sense of belonging and companionship. Given that Leo is immunocompromised, my socialization has been relegated to quick texts, outdoor coffees on a limited basis, and becoming comfortable with my social world taking a back seat to his treatment schedule and daily appointments. Peace, for me, comes in the knowledge that I have a wonderful circle of devoted men in my life who I could call if I need anything at all. Those relationships are not subject to seasonality; they just change in shape and form based on the circumstances.

As a husband and father, exhibiting **Gentle Strength** has become a challenge for me right now. My anxiety has been higher at baseline than at any other time in my life. The changes in my schedule, work-life balance, and relationship have been difficult to adjust to. As a result, my ability to be a soft landing for my wife and daughter has been more limited than usual. For Giovanna, to address the recent limits on our time together, I've made our weekly dates longer, more planful, and even multidimensional. Once-a-week breakfasts have evolved to become once-a-month trips to Six Flags, or five-stop "Tours of New Haven." Shifts in my approach have helped me convey to my daughter that she is seen and cared for, and to prioritize the time that she needs.

As a husband, my life and relationship have changed dramatically now that my son is very sick. I've had to work hard to be more selfless than at any other time in my adult life. It's essential for me to see my wife where she is on her journey. It's been incredibly challenging for her mentally and emotionally to watch her son suffer. Personally, I haven't done a great job of being patient, maintaining calmness and consistency, and being gentle. I've had to seek her grace and apologize, both often and well, when I snap or exhibit irritability. Her willingness to be patient with me in the face of my own personal difficulties demonstrates her care for me and willingness to afford me the benefit of the doubt.

Although my sons and I **Found Our Thing,** loving that thing looks very different now. Leo has obviously had to sit out this whole football season, which was the most difficult thing for him to give up of all that he's lost. Now, immersing ourselves in his thing is sitting in his hospital room, grinding two straight days of College Football followed by the NFL on Sunday, made possible by the ingenuity of his mother, who set up a projector and screen so that we could watch the game on a six-by-six screen. For Vince, it's him calling me to tell me that he just threw two touchdowns in last night's game, the first game he's ever played in his life that I've missed, but that he's dedicated those touchdowns to his brother. For me, it's not being their football coach anymore, though I'll be spending all day Monday in the hospital breaking down Vince's game tape, sending him tips and feedback on each play on both sides of the ball. Now, my job is to coach these young men in life. I'm coaching Leo every day on how to maintain a positive attitude in the face of illness and encouraging him to develop a vision for victory by imagining what his future will someday look like. For his brother, it's helping him manage his life, the relationships he is building, and how he makes decisions both on and off the field. Not being their football coach has left a void in me, but it's been a place we've filled with the relationship that we share with one another.

Works in progress

Life is a series of seasons, vacillating between the peaks and valleys. My son's life-threatening illness has demonstrated to me that although I found myself living in a period of bliss and comfort, it couldn't be like that forever. That season was merely a momentary payoff, the spoils that existed for a blink of an eye as a result of years of turmoil that I persevered through. I hope that I won't take that period for granted as I move forward in search of my next mountaintop. If history is any indicator, I'll find my way to another one, alongside my family and friends.

But, in reflecting upon the final words of this book—the sum total of the lessons that I've learned and hope to share with men, young men, and their families—I've found that what matters most is how we use the lessons that we have learned through experience to navigate the difficult seasons in our lives. Wisdom comes through the recognition that we are forever works in progress, and that what we know must be deployed differently based on the season in which we find ourselves. Using these lessons the right way will determine our ability to succeed in confronting whatever challenges we face.

ACKNOWLEDGMENTS

To the God of the universe who blessed me with all that I am, all that I have, and all that I've ever known: Thank you for all of it, even the parts that I didn't know how you would use until much later.

To G, my better half: Thank you for loving me for all that I am and all that I am not. Thank you for walking with me through every step of this insane road that has been our story. Thank you for the good years, the bad years, and the in-between years. Thank you for demanding more of me than I ever could have imagined of myself.

To my oldest son, Vince: Thank you for your character, your moral compass, and for your ability to do hard things. Never waver in your ability to identify and do what is right and to show up Big when it matters most.

To my son, Leo: Thank you for your light, for your fire, for your gravitas, and for the way that you inspire others. God has put a calling on your life. Continue to use your powers of influence for good, always.

To my Boo-Boo Bear, Giovanna: Thank you for our time together, for softening my heart, and for all of our dates and our fun little adventures. Thank you for showing us all how to be brave, even if you're small, and especially when it's hard. May your ferocity, intelligence, drive, and heart for serving people reward you in whatever you choose to bless this world with.

To Grandpa Harry: Thank you for teaching me to believe in myself before I was ready to.

To Grandma Minnie: Thank you for making me laugh and helping me to find comfort in simple pleasures.

To GG: Thank you for finding my soulmate and setting this adventure in motion.

To my father: Thank you for getting a lot of things right along the way and clearly demonstrating to me that I was wrong.

To Bobby and Jo: Thank you for opening your hearts, your home, and your life to a boy who wasn't quite ready to be a man. Thank you for seeing something in me, and for sharing with me your greatest gift and trusting that I could handle that responsibility. Thank you for the love and care you continue to show my family and me every day.

To Vinny and Vic: Thank you for your brotherhood and sisterhood, the likes of which know no words. Thank you for being role models to our family. And for merging your lives with our own.

To Sara and Frank: Thank you for showing us all a unique and different path and setting an example for my children that demonstrates loudly that their dreams can be as big as they can imagine.

To Ralphy: Thank you for being part of our family and for all the days, nights, and hours that you've spent with us that made our children better people.

To Zizi Greg: Thank you for bringing God into my life.

To Kim: Thank you for believing in me and for seeing the vision long before I ever could.

To the Causeway Team: Thank you for the way that you have poured everything you have into this mission for the last fourteen years. Thank you for your collective sacrifice, for your commitment to the cause, and for pushing the boundaries of what is possible at every turn. Thank you for leaving things better than you found them and for your willingness to carry out the journey on the road ahead. Thank you all for the opportunity to work alongside all of you over the years. Thank you for the lessons learned, for the wisdom gained, for the friendships forged, and for the privilege of supporting young men in building more meaningful lives.

To Bobby: Thank you for a lifelong friendship, and for making lifelong friends of our wives and children as well.

To Meg: Thank you for becoming part of our family and for holding it down with the kids for so many years. You enabled us to do what we needed.

To Eva and Angelo and Co.: Thank you for everything you have given us, for growing with us, and for raising our families alongside one another.

To Anna and Taryn: Thank you for being my sisters, for giving me the benefit of the doubt (when I didn't deserve it), and for trying to be objective (despite collectively knowing that G is always right).

VINCE BENEVENTO, LPC, is a licensed counselor in both New York and Connecticut, a husband, father, speaker, and entrepreneur. He holds a BA from Wesleyan University and a master's degree in School Counseling from Fairfield University. Vince possesses nearly twenty years of experience working specifically with men and young men as a coach, mentor, and therapist. The organization Vince founded and has directed for the last fifteen years, Causeway Collaborative, has supported over two thousand men and young men between the ages of fourteen and thirty, effectively changing the way that therapy has been done for guys who have been resistant to help. Now, Vince hopes to share key lessons with men (and those who love them) on how to become better versions of themselves.

www.ingramcontent.com/pod-product-compliance
Lightning Source LLC
LaVergne TN
LVHW010651110826
845149LV00014B/3027

9781959170310